Just Another Murder

Just Another Murder

෨෬

By CeCe Samal

WRITER'S PROOF

Published by Writer's Proof,
a division of Interview You, LLC
Athens, Georgia

www.justanothermurder.com

ISBN 0-9773365-1-4

Printed in the
United States of America

This book is dedicated to my daughters,
three beautiful and extraordinary women
whom I had the privilege of introducing to life.

Special thanks to my daughter Kris
for many hours of tireless work dedicated to
making this work complete.

Part I: The Seed Bed

Chapter One

On a beautiful Wednesday evening in the mid-seventies, my all-alone-orbit syndrome died. This is a condition which is perhaps peculiar to many widows. It is very real and strange.

While spinning in my own personal orbit, I was surrounded by creature comforts, as well as a lovely setting, and yet with a constant, inner, ceaseless ache. The ache was profound.

Although there was much to reach out to and touch, I did not reach out. It was like feeling alone on New Year's Eve in Times Square. Instead of reaching out, I elected to retreat into the Land of Nod.

Now I understand that I had a very real need that perhaps only those that have been in the situation can understand. In any event, on this magical night in February, the spinning stopped and the symptoms of the syndrome disappeared due to a chance encounter on my way to prayer meeting.

On this balmy winter evening in Ft. Lauderdale, Florida, an incident occurred which changed my life forevermore.

ഔരൂ

With Bible in hand, I set out for the Wednesday evening prayer meeting at the First Baptist Church, located on the corner of Broward Boulevard and Third Avenue. Because I was an hour early and time permitted, I opted to go for coffee at Howard Johnson's restaurant, which was just a few blocks away.

To me, as a widow, "Ho Jo's" represented a secure place to be. Actually, there was a particular stool at the far end of the counter which I claimed as my own. This location afforded a panoramic view of the establishment with everything and everyone in sight, a security measure that had become second nature in my widowhood.

As I approached "my" stool, I noticed flatware and a glass of water at "my" spot. However, after a moment's reflection, I decided to sit there anyway and ordered coffee. A few moments later I was aware of a young man standing next to me. I looked at him and said, "Oh, I'm sorry, is this your seat?" He very gallantly said it was all right and took the stool to my right.

A mental picture of his attire that night – the white embroidered shirt and terrific legs clad in white jeans – remains etched on my mind. He wore boots. His 6-foot 2-inch frame, deep-set blue eyes in a soft-featured, sometimes rugged face and extremely good looks were enticing. I dared not or would not consciously admit that here was a most desirable combination.

"Doc," as he wished to be called, had ordered fried clams. He asked me to join him, and I settled for a hamburger. As our conversation continued, I noticed his voice was soft, and he had charm. His speech was descriptive, and he used southern colloquial expressions in illustrating his points. Almost immediately I noticed Doc's imagination was remarkable, and in one sentence he could span space and mountains. Whether his stories were fact or fiction, I did not know. I only know I enjoyed listening to him.

My guard was down, and I offered to take him to check for sleeping accommodations as he had just arrived in town. Doc paid the check, and then with a flourish, presented the waitress with a five-dollar tip.

We left Ho Jo's and walked to my sports car, a neat yellow and black Firebird Esprit with a 360 engine. This represented a lot of power.

Actually, this day was an historical one for me. On this same day, in the afternoon, I sat on the same stool and struck up a conversation with another young man. It wasn't very long before we realized we shared a mutual interest in writing. Therefore, I invited him to my home that evening to continue our discussion.

This was an absolute first for me as I had not extended an invitation to anyone in this manner since I had been widowed almost two years before. My house had become my security blanket, and I guarded my privacy. Consequently, I was bewildered by this unprecedented invitation I had offered. Nevertheless, the deed was done, and the date had been set for the nine o'clock hour so that I could attend prayer meeting.

After the initial shock of the realization that I had, in fact, invited a virtual stranger to my home registered, I placed a call to my daughter Susan. Just to be safe, I asked if she and her husband, Larry, would casually stop by the house and check out the situation.

The apprehension I felt was incredible. A male and a stranger coming to my house! Just to play it safe, a few more phone calls were placed with an invitation for the nine o'clock hour, even though I was not sure the stranger would show up.

In the meantime, with the prayer meeting forgotten, Doc and I rode around to several motels. We began with the Marina Inn on the Causeway and cruised around and then on down South Federal Highway. Just beyond the airport a rooster was standing outside the door of a small bar, called Michael's, and the rooster crowed. The scene amused me, and I wondered if it held some special significance. My awareness of all about me was heightened, and everything seemed brighter, filled with significance.

After further inquiries, we decided Ft. Lauderdale was devoid of rental rooms. (Tourist season was in full swing.) At this point I decided I needed to head for home as the nine o'clock hour was drawing near.

As we drove up to my house, Doc noticed my bike in the carport. He asked, "Do you have kids?" I replied, "Yes, but they do not live here." (There are three daughters, married and on their own.) Later in our relationship, it turned out that Doc thought that I was younger than my years, and I imagined him to be older than he proved to be.

As I have always held chronological time at arm's length, never wanting to be put in a category according to my age, I really did not think in terms of his age or mine. More-over, the coming of age in my thoughts – going forward and reversing itself – chronological timing was never in my heart, and as a result I sometimes had trouble in my thinking of going beyond sixteen years of age.

Meanwhile, the group that gathered at my house at precisely nine o'clock was rather unusual. Most of those present were strangers to each another. There was Doc Foxx, who presented himself as a country-boy hillbilly from Georgia and Tennessee; Bill Bronsen, a tall, thin potential writer; and Tammy Logan, a lovely, young, dark-haired woman who possessed writing aspirations and had come to return a book to me. Tammy was accompanied by a male friend. And, according to plan, Susan and Larry dropped by in the event I might need to be rescued.

Behind the nice, calm exterior of this home in Ft. Lauderdale, the gathering that took place seems to have been the beginning of a myriad of experiences that became the inagural events of a new phase of my life.

The group was congenial, and I found myself concentrating on Doc. In the most friendly and pleasant manner I could muster, I did my best to encourage my guests to leave. Soon, Bill, Doc and I were a threesome. Then I began centering all my efforts on disposing of Bill so that I could concentrate solely on Doc. Bill kept resisting, but soon my persistence worked, and Bill departed.

Around midnight, Doc and I were alone in my home, creating a scene that was totally foreign to the solitary way I had been living for nearly two years now.

Although I was active, attending classes at the local community college and studying, the remainder of my time was spent indulging myself, spinning in my all -alone orbit. This orbit had been the essence of my world for so long! It was a world where I was often hurt and confused, unable to get comfortable enough to move on and find new meaning for my life.

Although it outwardly appeared that I had it "all together," it was not so . . . until now.

On this very special night when the souls of two strangers touched, I took the first faltering step toward returning to the mainstream of life.

On this momentous night, I heard myself saying, "Since it is so late and I have extra bedrooms, you can stay here, but just for tonight."

There were two bedrooms and a bath on one side of the house, which was divided by the living room and dining area. The master bath and bedroom were on the opposite side. I offered Doc the bedroom with the single bed and pointed out the bathroom.

Finally, I said goodnight, and went into the master bedroom and closed the door. My very next act was to lock the door, and then push a small bureau against it. Next, having settled in my bed, I reflected for a long time on the fact that I had a stranger, a male, alone with me in the house.

The next morning Doc left. My son-in-law Larry had planned to come over and help me move furniture, as I had scheduled an appointment for new furniture delivery.

In the early afternoon, Larry had arrived and was in the bedroom preparing to remove a bureau when the phone rang. It was Doc. Doc told me he had secured a room at the Governors' Club Hotel in downtown Ft. Lauderdale. He then asked me if I would come to the hotel and meet him in the lobby. I agreed. I felt excited.

As I rather frantically tried to determine what to wear, it became a session of selecting, trying on and discarding one outfit after another. Each selection was either too tight or unsuitable for the occasion.

Finally, I decided on a two-piece, pajama-type midriff costume (and support panty hose). This fabric was a green floral print, and the top had full three-quarter sleeves. Thankfully, my mid-section was shown off to advantage, since it was exposed. In my mind, I resolved, on the spot, to lose weight. Where do those extra bulges come from so suddenly?

Feelings that had been dormant for a long time began to surface as I drove to the hotel. Within moments I was parked in the lot behind the hotel. As I entered the lobby, Doc walked over to greet me with a grin which conveyed much delight. Doc looked terrific. He was wearing medium-blue denim jeans with silver studs on the outside seams, and a shirt also decorated with silver studs. He made a striking appearance and several strangers complimented him. The black high-heeled boots he was wearing enhanced his great legs and added to the total picture. Doc's blue eyes were so blue; his sandy hair was combed so that it fell slightly over his forehead.

Doc handed me a package wrapped in blue and tied with a silver ribbon. Nervous excitement came over me as I opened the package and discovered a sterling silver I.D. bracelet with my name engraved on it. The card read "Thanks for your hospitality. Doc."

This gesture of gratitude fostered a precious moment, something I had not allowed in my life for a long time.

Doc was asking me to come upstairs as he wanted me to see his room. At first I said it wasn't a good idea. Although I had been to the hotel dining room, and also the banquet room, this was the extent of my knowledge of the hotel.

The hotel was an old establishment which had been considered quite elegant and had, in fact, housed royalty. It was evident that Doc was impressed with his room, and he persisted in his pleas that I see the room. Finally, I consented. However, the room was quite simple, but through Doc's eyes it became a tour resplendent. Truly, it was all in the eye of the beholder.

As Doc attempted to embrace me, I, of course, eluded his playful advances. Obviously, I had to. The several invisible "do not disturb" and "no trespassing" signs which were firmly adhered to me could not be violated.

Miami Beach and The Rascal House were decided upon as the next best activity of the day. Once in the car, our hands accidentally touched on the gear shift. Instantly, electric vibrations pulsed through both of us like a million lightning streaks that established an extraordinary chemistry.

As we drove down A1A there was a great deal of road construction apparent, which is typical for south Florida during the busy winter season. Doc proved to be a good driver. At one point the Firebird overheated, and he handled the problem easily, with great dexterity.

Once we arrived at the Rascal House, we delighted in the lively atmosphere. The bowls of coleslaw and pickles and all the extra specialties of the house were a treat.

The spell that was woven by the excitement of our developing friendship was magical, and the relationship seemed so natural.

On the return trip, Doc reached over to take my hand, and the electric sensation returned with a trembling vengeance.

That evening as I attended my class at Broward Community College, I displayed the gift I had received from Doc. The gift really impressed a friend, and she said, "Wow, and all that from one guy!" I also shared with her my experiences of the day.

As Doc and I had agreed to meet that evening, I could not wait for the class to be over. Therefore, I left early, never stopping to consider what was happening to me. I was elated with a sense of adventure and a new high, a feeling of coming back to life.

That night we decided to go to the Bahia Mar beach to go swimming. I completely forgot that ocean night swimming was a no-no for me. Nor did the slight chill of the evening register. My only concern was the consideration of what bathing suit to wear: a two-piece number or the one-piece Italian suit that really looked great and also had the illusion of see-through. The one-piece suit was my choice, and I felt good.

The Bahia Mar area is a wide expanse of beach, and we happily romped and splashed and ducked in the surf. We were caught up in a great sensation of being in our own world. At one point Doc picked me up with ease and carried me over to a picnic bench. An invisible web of enchantment had surely been spun around our two figures as we talked, absorbed in the beauty of the evening.

Later that evening, alone in my home, I began reflecting on the events that were transpiring in my life.

My thinking led me to decide that it would be a good idea to invite Doc to visit my college campus, specifically to introduce him to young female students.

The next day, Doc and I set out for the Broward Community College main campus. This school had much meaning to me. This world of academia was a place in which I could function well. To me, it was a safe place, a place where I could feel comfortable as who were there and I shared a common purpose.

This visit proved a fun time as I introduced Doc around. However, I did not push the idea of his helping him meet young female students, and I did not consider why.

The shift and change in my life had been sudden. My reaction to this sudden change was that I began to tell Doc to get lost and go find someone else to date. It seems I could not quite cope with allowing myself to be embraced by so much attention.

Doc did get lost – for two days. He returned to say he had met a girl walking her dog on the beach in the early morning dawn. She was nice, but he was just not interested.

The following morning I found a note attached to my mailbox which read, "Hi, Honey. Look in your box. I have something to give to you with my love. I hope you like it. I do love you so much. Love, Doc."

The gift was a gold necklace with profile silhouettes of a boy and girl kissing. Of course, it all conveyed a sweet message.

Suddenly, Doc was always there. He raked and cleaned the yard. In the backyard he took a two-by-four and with the side of his hand, hit the board and broke it evenly in two. And I was impressed. The suggestion that I would like a front section of the house painted resulted in a willing volunteer. As he painted, he would look in through the picture window, always grinning. Doc used the term "honey" with ease. Two of my daughters happened by, and when they heard him call me "honey" and "baby," became a bit upset and asked what was going on here.

Of all things, the paint was maroon, nevertheless, Doc just laughed as the paint splashed on his white trousers. Later I got busy trying to remove the stains but, alas, to no avail. Later that same day, Doc left. He was gone for two days. I called the Governors' Club Hotel and was told he had checked out. So much for this friendship. Despite this, later this same day, Doc called to say he had passed out on the street two nights before . . . and had been taken to Broward General Hospital.

I then said, "You should have let me know." Doc said he had gone to stay with his cousin Steve who also lived in Ft. Lauderdale. There was, as I would later discover, a great network of "kin." Another consequence of this episode was the loss, for Doc, of a huge roll of cash and also a gorgeous jewel-encrusted cross Doc was wearing when I met him. Jewelry was important to Doc, as was clothing, and he wore the cross with his shirt unbuttoned midway.

The following afternoon as I was taking a tennis lesson at the South Side Tennis Courts, I looked toward the street and saw Doc standing there watching me. Later that same day Doc called, and we talked for a long time. When I mentioned that I felt uneasy in the house alone, he said he would call later that evening and check on me.

This fear, being afraid when alone in the house at night, had become a neurosis, an unconscious nursing of the presence of an embodiment of unseen fear, which had become a companion to me. This unseen presence was very real to me.

The ringing of the phone at 1:30 a.m. ordinarily

would have caused me to panic, but this early a.m. I felt rather smug. I knew who was calling. Doc was checking to see if all was well. In our phone conversation I had indicated that I felt uneasy. It was not long after this that I heard steps around my walkway. He had walked all the way from downtown in just a short time to look around and make certain that all was well. I turned over in my bed with a new feeling of happiness and protection wrapped around me. At this moment, the fear that I had been entertaining quietly tiptoed out.

The Royal Castle restaurant, on the corner of Davie Blvd. and Riverland Road, in time, became a haven of fun and friends for Doc and me. it was convenient as it was about eight blocks from my house. One evening he was helping out, a generous spur-of-the-moment decision.

On this particular evening we had a dinner date. I waited at home and as the appointed time passed, my growing impatience got the better of me. I began to feel let down. The idea of being escorted to dinner was very attractive to me.

I got into my car and drove to Royal Castle. Doc said the date would have to be delayed as he was still "helping out." I became angry, and as I took off from the parking lot, I really spun my wheels.

Later, Doc came to my house, and we decided to go to the movies. "Shampoo" starring Warren Beatty was playing at the mall on State Road Seven. The theater was stifling, and Doc left once or twice for a period of time. Of course, I let him know that I did not appreciate this and considered it rude. In addition, the movie made me feel uncomfort-able. To me, this movie was on a par with "The Graduate," and introduced some controversial scenes that, to me, were embarrassing. (One of my daughter's high school boyfriends had once accused me of being a "Puritan from New England" as he knew I had come from Connecticut. This boyfriend felt my standards concerning my daughter were too strict.) After the movie, as we walked to the car which was parked some distance away, the subject of age came up.

Doc asked me if I were in my thirties. I said, "No."

He then said, "You're not in your forties, are you?"

I replied, "I can't help when I was born. You're not going to hold it against me, are you?"

At first he looked incredulous and upon reflection said what a terrific pair we would have made if I had been born sooner and he had been born later in a different point and place in time. In spite of this, somehow, it didn't seem to make any difference.

Chapter Two

Suddenly, I was no longer alone. Life, for me, took on a new dimension. The days and nights were filled with adventure and fun. Strangely, this new excitement was accompanied by a self-consciousness I could not explain.

One perfect evening as Doc and I walked along the broad walkway on Hollywood Beach, we were oblivious to the many folks also enjoying this place, this place that I had come to so many times in my aloneness, this place that I so often had run to after my husband's death when immersed in thoughts which created pain that I could not erase.

My husband was the person with whom I had shared many years building a family life. Together we had three beautiful daughters and shared the wonderful happiness and agony that the challenge of a family living and building in love and sharing can produce.

And now, here I was, elated, in this same place with Doc, who, with his electrifying energy and enthusiasm, was taking one stride to my two steps. As I tried to keep up with his fast pace, I realized I was enthralled with his conversation.

Doc was spinning tales about his life in Georgia and Tennessee and about his "granny," his "mama," and his "grandaddy" on his mother's side. As we walked hand-in-hand, I was looking up at Doc and listening and laughing and wishing I had a colloquial dictionary to interpret and clarify some of the expressions he used. Doc had acquired pure Elizabethan expressions such as "look yonder." Much of his speech was refreshingly different.

Being called a "foxy lady" was new to me. Since I was not familiar with the term, I asked my son-in-law, David Bridges, what it meant. David explained that it was quite a compliment. He said, "It means he thinks you're special and attractive and sexy."

I replied, "Oh, I just was not sure what it meant." Of course, I was pleased and flattered.

Being called "honey" and "baby" was nice. However, when we were in a restaurant and Doc referred to a waitress as "honey," I didn't think it was so nice. Of course, I told him I considered this tacky and lacking in refinement. In my New England frame of reference, this sort of allusion was reserved for use by truck drivers. Thereafter, his "honey" and "baby" were exclusively for me.

As we spent more and more time with each other, we visited with friends and relatives in the area. My brother Art and his wife, Elia, maintained a winter residence at the Point of Americas, a condominium apartment on the beach. Art liked Doc, and this pleased me. As my older brother, one of four actually, I adored Art as I was growing up, so his opinion was important to me. Art was delighted that I was happy and having fun, for, he said, "You're much too young to be left alone."

And the DeLeo's, Ed and Verdi, the most precious friends I could have, were happy for me, as well. Ed had worked with my husband. As surrogate members of my family, Ed and Verdi were aware of and sensitive to the trauma I had endured in my life.

Also, my dear friend Gerry and her husband, Al, were people who had been involved with my family through the years. As dear friends, their opinion was important to me, too. They were delighted for me in my new-found friendship with Doc.

Chapter Three

One day Doc and I decided to visit my Aunt Lydia in Venice, located on the west coast of Florida. We traveled on Alligator Alley, and when we arrived on the west end of this highway, we went into Sambo's restaurant.

Doc, with his height and build, was an imposing figure in an army fatigue jacket and boots, dark-mirrored glasses and paratrooper's emblem. As he walked, he held himself in a military stance. Added to this, he greeted folks with the peace sign.

This image seemed to infuriate some of the guests in the restaurant on this particular morning. A few of these same people freely called us "capitalistic pigs."

The warmth of our welcome when we arrived at my Aunt Lydia's home was a great contrast to the atmosphere in Sambo's. Lydia, my dear, lovely Swedish aunt, was my mother's sister and although I had seen her infrequently through the years, we shared a beautiful closeness. Aunt Lydia's Swedish accent was charming as were the sparkle and twinkle in her eyes that she could not contain when she met Doc.

Later, at lunch, Aunt Lydia confided that she would do the same romantic thing if she were younger and had the opportunity. She thought my being with Doc was wonderful. After we concluded the visit, we enjoyed a pleasant, fun ride across the state, heading for the east coast and A1A. Although we covered a lot of miles, it seemed like a short drive.

"My Eyes Adored You" was popular then and became our song. As we drove along, Doc would sing and strum an imaginary guitar. Somehow, I could not convince Doc that he had a really good voice.

As we drove down A1A, life was a song. The beach

is, of course, an exquisitely romantic place to be. We stopped when we arrived at Lauderdale-by-the-Sea, and we walked on the beach.

The sights of nature and people always conjured up conversation. Doc described "red necks" as wearing bobby socks and drinking Blue Ribbon beer. Invariably, an incident would occur which would seem to prove his point. Voilá – magic!

After a walk on the beach, we came back by way of the sidewalk. What was it that made me pull back? Why was I awkwardly conscious of us as a couple? I fell back a few paces and Doc reached back and with his enormous hand, took mine and literally pulled me back into the mainstream of life. My confidence returned, and once again I felt reasonably comfortable.

The next day we visited a rug firm in Miami. Since Doc had experience in carpet laying, he wanted to pursue, possibly, a business in the area.

On the way to Miami on I-95, a huge eighteen-wheeler had jack-knifed at one of the exits. Traffic was backed up as a result. Doc jumped out of the car and proceeded to direct traffic and really got things moving like an expert. He looked so handsome as he stood out there in his white trousers and shirt. There was no doubt he was in command.

When the police arrived, everything was under control. They thanked him, and we left. Reacting the way he did was just part of his personality and demonstrated his capability in responding to emergency situations.

At the rug firm, as Doc explained the varieties of carpeting to me, the colors and materials seemed to come alive and were vibrant. Doc explained to the management that he was interested in starting in some phase of the business in the area. He also introduced me as his partner. Naturally, I was rather surprised and a bit flattered.

However, since I've never been interested in the business world, I did not take this seriously. It was just a game.

The man we spoke with did, indeed, seem to enjoy our visit. There was a noticeable twinkle in his eye. There was obviously something in our demeanor that was suggestive of romantic intrigue.

Day by day, as we were together more and more, Doc began staying over at the house. Somehow, I found this most agreeable. We began to develop friendships with groups of people who accepted us as a twosome.

At Royal Castle there was Bob, who worked the early evening shift. Bob was nice. And Larry, who worked the morning shift, was interesting. Larry was a prison parolee whose ex-wife was a policewoman on the Ft. Lauderdale police force. They had a little daughter whom Larry adored.

And then there was Dick. A most interesting fellow. Dick managed the midnight shift and was at all times willing to render a quick operatic performance in his deep baritone voice. Dick was bald on top and let the hair he had grow long, and this was visible from ear to ear. This length of hair was converted into a sort of Chinese tail. This friend was in his mid-thirties and was in Phi Theta Kappa, the academic honor fraternity at Broward Community College, as was I.

These folks were incorporated into the thread that was beginning to fashion a pattern in our lives. Larry would call in the morning and say, "Come on down, and I'll treat you to eggs and grits." Needless to say, this became a fun place to visit.

One evening Doc and I decided to visit my daughter Kris. Kris is a very beautiful blonde, a young woman of truly exemplary looks. Kris and David with their little blonde daughter, Laurie, lived in a duplex in Lauderhill.

As I believed Kris and David were interested in purchasing new carpeting, Doc brought along some carpet samples. Of course, the intention was to give them the whole package at cost.

When we arrived, two of my daughters were there. Somehow I sensed they were not too happy about Doc at this point. They seemed, in fact, a bit excited and overwrought. David, on the other hand, said to me, "What is wrong with the girls? Doc seems like a nice and decent guy to me." And, of course, he was.

Doc and Laurie got along famously. Doc was fond of children. He won Laurie's heart with his magic tricks.

On the other hand, the carpet samples didn't go over so well. The girls' suspicious, non-accepting attitudes prevailed.

Chapter Four

Shopping again! This was becoming a regular, fun activity. Doc was a jewelry enthusiast, and as he pointed out interesting pieces of jewelry, exploring jewelry counters and window shopping became alive and vivid. Clothes and guns and furniture as well as every other type of article took on new intrigue and fascination for me.

On one particular shopping trip at the Coral Ridge Mall, Doc was testing shaving equipment. As he was sampling the various electric shavers, he shaved off one of the long side burns he sported at the time. He just laughed and said, "I'm just a crazy guy." This was a happy-go-lucky attitude I grew to enjoy.

That day I bought a beautiful mirror with an ornate antique-gold frame. Doc picked up the mirror, which was large and heavy, and carried it as easily as though it were a notebook!

Curiosity caused me to wonder, and I said "Doc, surely you must have shopped with other women?"

"No," he replied, "I never have."

As I was typically a lone shopper, this "share shopping" was new to me. Surprisingly, I found I enjoyed it.

The following afternoon in the kitchen of my home, Doc was extemporaneously performing karate chops and motions that he was quite adept at. He then tried to kiss me and succeeded on the third try. He then laughed and said incredulously, "You don't know how to kiss!" Although I wasn't quite sure of what he meant, I managed to show indignation.

Suddenly, Doc was aware that a seam on his jeans had split. The split was down the side of the fly opening. I got out a needle and thread and went into the family room.

Here was this macho guy holding both his big hands over the split. He was as red as a beet and was walking with legs close together, crossing one in front of the other. As he had to remove his jeans, he sat with a towel wrapped around himself as he sewed the seam.

Later, Doc sat at the table and with one finger on my portable typewriter, he picked out the message, "I love CeCe, and she will become Mrs. James A. Foxx III." I laughed at what I considered a rather incredible prospect, however intriguing, as I had vowed never to marry again.

Tattooed on Doc's upper left arm was the name Sue. On his right hand and wrist area and above was a cross that read Jesus. On his left wrist he wore a rather large chain-link bracelet. It was a permanent fixture as it was welded together.

On this same afternoon I stated that I considered tattoos rather vulgar. I had recently read that people who displayed tattoos were not to be trusted. My dislike for this form of art work as well as the idea of Doc's "wearing" another woman's name on his person combined to make the tatoo on his arm an issue for me. I told him that the name had to go.

Doc went out and purchased some India ink and a large needle, and with this equipment changed the name to mine. He then informed me the tattoos had been an immeasurable source of comfort to him in the jungles of Viet Nam.

"Doc" was the name James assumed when he arrived in Florida. He certainly had a vast knowledge of the medical field, and he claimed to have been an army medic. The name suited him. This simple country boy apparently had an intricately complex aspects whose parts surfaced periodically.

Quite suddenly, Doc announced that he needed to go to Georgia as his "mama" was ill. Mama had left Daddy when Doc was quite young. I learned that Doc had an older sister. His mother had remarried and another son was born of this marriage. This division left quite a psychological impact on Doc's life, I eventually discovered. "Granny" was the most significant frame of family reference. It was easy to gather that Doc adored Granny.

As Doc checked into reservations for the trip to Georgia, I suggested that I was ready for a trip and would consider driving to Georgia with him. We left for Georgia shortly thereafter.

An interesting encounter was a brief interlude with my daughters and their husbands. They had scheduled a meeting at a Ramada Inn in Central Florida as they were involved in college meetings in the area that week. We all met midway in their motel suite.

An additional aspect of the trip for me was that, when we left Ft. Lauderdale, I had a slight bladder infection. It grew steadily worse as the trip progressed.

When we arrived at our destination, Doc wanted to take me to meet Granny immediately. What a grand lady she was! Doc had purchased a gift of a bouquet of artificial flowers. After the initial introductions were performed, Doc held the bouquet behind his back and then with a grand gesture presented it to Granny. She was delighted! Doc knew her so well.

Granny had been instrumental in caring for Doc when he was a youngster. She managed to instill a good value system in Doc while caring for him.

At this place, there were, it seemed, children coming out of the woodwork. Granny took care of her daughter's several children. There was a collection of other relatives' children, as well. It seems Granny's calling in life was to bring love and attention to what might otherwise have been a regrettable situation.

In spite of her tenderness, there was another side of

her personality that Doc loved to tell about. At times when Granny would become angry, she would pile her hair on top of her head and spin around three times using an Indian expression, and everyone knew she was serious and you'd best get out of the way. Doc relished this aspect of Granny's nature.

When Granny and I met, there was instant mutual admiration and respect transmitted between us.

The younger children were asking for money. It rather shocked me to see the little ones smoking. The cigarettes looked larger than they did. Granny was distressed by the smoking. However, she had no control over this habit once it became ingrained. Pee Wee, a precocious youngster, was very small, as her name implied, and had been a chain smoker at a tender age.

In any event, the people and the setting in Georgia held an allure for me. I really liked it, and I liked Granny, Glenis, cousin Tommy (a handsome guy who might conceivably pass for Doc's twin except for Tommy's dark hair), and the assortment of children who were blessed with a gift for affection. All of this brought a lovely sense of joy.

Later, Doc secured a place at the Pines Motel. It consisted of three rooms – a bedroom, a living room and a kitchenette – not to mention a back porch and clothesline. And, amazingly, the price was right.

It was not long before Doc mentioned he'd like to visit his mother. Actually, I was glad to have some time to myself. After he left, I went across the street for a bite to eat. While seated at the counter, I found myself surrounded by much friendliness. In fact, I was invited to several events including a "pot" party. Enough! I returned to the Pines, grateful for a chance to rest as my bladder infection wasrather painful.

Doc returned in the early a.m. after having been gone for many hours. He remained in the living room with a person identified as "Butterford" who was also kin. "Butterford" was, to paraphrase Mark Twain, "soiled and seedy and fragrant with the weed." This was still another scene foreign to my lifestyle, and I did not appreciate being a part of this tableau.

Doc was concerned for his sister as she was in the process of divorcing her husband and consequently in an unhappy state of mind. Doc had spent hours trying to locate her, and we continued looking but did not find her that morning. Later, he did locate her. I liked her very much. She was tall and quite slim with dark hair. Doc said, "If she stood behind a telephone pole, you couldn't see her." There was much good-natured affection between them. Although she teased him, there was no doubt she was proud of him.

The next day I decided it was time for me to leave. Actually, I had thought about leaving on my own before this. However, the bladder infection I was nursing kept me partially incapacitated, and so I waited.

Before we left, Doc wanted to drive past his maternal grandparent's house. Evidently, there was a division in the family. This side of the family was aloof from the others I had recently met. For some reason, Doc held these grandparents in great awe and felt unworthy to grace their doorstep.

We left and headed south via I-75. It was rather perplexing to me to see people waving to Doc in pleasant recognition.

Soon I realized that Doc was not altogether happy with the idea of leaving now. Therefore, I made the suggestion that he go back until he could be more definite as to where he wanted to be.

We exited I-75, and Doc pulled into a gas station and

parked on the side of the building. The station had not yet opened. It was a chilly morning in Georgia, and he sat there reflecting on the situation. I became impatient. "Make up your mind," I said, "either keep on going or get out and go back." He gathered up his things and seemed hesitant and undecided. Undoubtedly, I had forced the issue. I slipped into the driver's seat and started the car. As I took off down the road, I waved "bye bye."

Why did I feel so right about this? Whatever the reason, the feeling was one of elation.

As I drove down into Florida with this marvelous, pleased feeling, I suddenly realized I was devoid of cash. Doc had been holding "our" cash. Soon I sighted a Welcome Station and there learned it was impossible to cash a personal check.

As I approached Gainesville, I stopped at the first bank I came to. Again, I was told there was no possible way they would cash a personal check. The teller then asked me if I had a Visa card as there was a bank in town that would lend me money on the strength of the card. I arrived at that bank just a few moments before its closing time.

When asked how much money I wished to have, I replied, "Ten dollars will be fine." However, I was then in-formed I could not take less than twenty-five dollars. "Great!" I said, "That will do nicely."

As I drove down the Sunshine State Turnpike, I felt light and free. My car sailed along and was inclined to do ninety miles an hour most of the time. My mind fully an-ticipated that a highway patrolman would stop me; however, somehow I was overlooked.

Later that evening, after arriving home, I went to Royal Castle. It was Bob's shift, and he asked, "Where's Doc?" I proceeded to tell him the whole story and said, "I dumped

Doc in Georgia, and I guess that is the end of our friendship."
Bob said much to assure me that Doc would return. He was
very positive of this as he said he knew Doc.

At home again I felt good, and surprisingly was not
afraid to be alone in the house. It was a good feeling.

Since my husband's death, I seldom cooked. And
here and now, at this late hour, I began cooking . . . just in
case.

The evening was especially lovely, and I walked outside several times to check. Somehow I had been entertaining
the expectation of a "guest." It was a delicious sensation of
expectation without any solid foundation. To try to analyze
these feelings simply produced an emotional high.

Chapter Five

Phone calls started the next day. Doc called from
Georgia to say he would be returning to Ft. Lauderdale. Since
he was hitch-hiking, he would call each time he was between
rides and near an available phone. At one point he received a
pink warning slip from a highway patrolman on the Florida
Turnpike. In addition, there were also other propositions of
another variety that, he said, were offered and refused.

Late that evening, the last phone call of the day announced that Doc had arrived. Doc was calling from the
7-11 convenience store on Davie Blvd. The store was just a
few blocks away. Doc was standing outside the store. As I
drove up, he walked over to the car and said, "I'm cold." The
trip had obviously been very trying. Nevertheless, it seemed
so natural to be with him again.

Later, we drove down to Royal Castle, and Larry and
Bob and the others in the place gave us a "royal" welcome.
Bob said, "I told you he'd be back."

Indeed he was. Doc said the moment I drove off that
morning in Georgia he regretted getting out of the car as he
knew then he wanted to be with me.

Marriage was on Doc's mind. He said, "Because
I know you wouldn't consider living with me without the
sanctity of marriage, please marry me." I told him it wouldn't
work. And, after all, I had said I would never remarry after
my husband's death. Then I came up with the suggestion
that we remain friends and possibly meet once a month,
perhaps at a resort or some interesting rendevous. Doc would
not even consider this proposition.

Every moment Doc remained an interesting, exciting
person. He loved to bring me surprises, 'just to see the expres-

sion on my face," as he put it. He brought me presents, such as a hanging basket of flowers, jewelry, fancy drinking glasses, sets of cut-glass salt and pepper shakers, and all kinds of gifts. He also had a habit of exaggerating the price of these tokens of affection, which simply made the gestures all the more precious.

In spite of the vast differences in our cultural background, we had much in common we could relate to. One very basic tenet was our religious belief in Jesus. A Baptist, I had been baptized at the age of twelve. Doc had undoubtedly been taken to church by Granny and also the foster parents he had lived with as a youngster.

With all of Doc's strengths, he possessed magnificent tenderness as well as good manners, always showing gratitude for little things. The few times I did prepare a meal for him, he never failed to say, "Thank you for the delicious meal."

The mutual faith we shared solidified our growing bond of friendship. My faith was my fortress in the deep trials I had experienced in my life. There were times when I could say with conviction as Job did, "though He slay me, yet will I trust Him."

With the suggestion of marriage in the air, I began to search my Bible for an answer concerning the difference in our ages. What I discovered was, in fact, the Bible alluded to many unusual situations regarding age. There was nothing indicating an age difference like ours mattered. And it was only after I had cried out to the Lord in prayer, much as His child, saying, "Lord, you know my very real needs, and I'm trusting You to supply them," that Doc had appeared in my life.

There were other situations to be prayed about. For instance, Doc had instigated a law suit based on a job-related injury he had suffered while working in Cuba for a construction company. (Doc passing out on the street in Fort Lauderdale was the result of the injury sustained on the job in Cuba.)

A workman's compensation lawyer, assumed to be the best and located in Miami, had been secured for the case after a consultation with my attorney.

Next, a rather bizarre series of events developed. Doc was advised to see a particular doctor in Ft. Lauderdale who specialized in these cases. At the initial visit and upon examination, Doc was informed that a complicated operation was in order. The operation would involve removal and replacement of hip and leg bones with plastic facsimiles. Patients in the waiting room all seemed so grateful for their treatment. Also, I could not help noticing it all seemed so disabling.

Due to the fact the accident had taken place in Cuba and the company was denying Doc's service with them, stating there was no record of his activity, the doctor refused to see Doc on his next scheduled appointment.

Although the first visit had been pleasant, the second visit was equivalent to "get thee hence," sans the insurance. Nevertheless, this proved fortunate. A blessing in disguise, as it were.

The next step was to gather proof of Doc's employment in Cuba. Doc had given me his I.D. pass and other proof of his Cuban experiences at Guantanamo Bay when I first met him. However, the proof required for the lawsuit was of a different nature.

Once again, marriage became a topic of conversation. Doc wanted to be married in May. He was counting on the settlement from the lawsuit and said it would be all mine.

When I told my daughter who lived in Georgia of our plans, she asked, "What's the rush?" She continued, "Surely, if it is worthwhile, it will keep for a while."

She is the mother of Jake, my beautiful, very special grandson. Jake loved Doc and called him "Grampa Doc."

I totally neglected to take notice of her suggestion. It was offered, after all, on a long distance phone call, and I was floating on cloud nine.

The guys at Royal Castle were delighted as were our friends, Ed and Verdi. There were others who were happy, too, such as my friend Rosie. Rosie was a black friend who had taken care of members of my family when they were patients in the hospital where she worked. Rosie called me "Mother," and she had the uncanny knack of making people laugh in spite of any condition. Rosie was ecstatic over the marriage announcement.

Shopping for wedding clothes was fun. I had purchased not one but two dresses for the wedding ceremony. Doc helped me select the dresses at a boutique in the Coral Ridge Mall.

His charisma was at work in this shop as several of the women customers began seeking his advice and attention with their clothing selections. Boy, I found this annoyed me no end. It would have been harmless to simply let these little episodes run their course. He did have good taste. But, after all, I wanted the attention.

The wedding date was set for May 18. My long time and dearest friend Gerry, with her husband Al, agreed to be our honor attendants. They were both filled with joy for us.

We purchased our wedding bands in a jewelry store on S.W. 1st Avenue downtown. We selected wide gold bands with our initials engraved in silver. They were quietly elegant.

Next on the agenda was the marriage license and the blood test. Although one may feel all is well, there seemed to be a certain amount of apprehension. We traveled to Miami for the tests. The Spanish person who took our applications gave me an incredulous look with raised brows. This, of course, was intended to convey a message to me. This attitude was quite a contrast to the waitress at the Marina Inn who joyfully called us "kids" and lit the candles, as she said, "to create a romantic setting" for our dinner.

A church ceremony was what we desired. I contacted the Reverend Harry Hutton of the Southwest Baptist Church on S.W. 9th Avenue. Rev. Hutton suggested pre-marriage counseling; however, I convinced him it was not necessary. Also, I assured him that I realized the circumstances were unusual, that I had fully researched the various aspects of the situation. Prayer was the avenue that led to my positive decision. And, I added, in any event, we would be married. At this point the Reverend quite graciously consented to perform the ceremony on the designated date.

The Rev. Hutton was a virtual stranger to me. Actually, I had totally avoided consulting my own pastor, the Rev. Steve Swanson of the First Baptist Church.

Reverend Swanson had also been a good family friend as well as our spiritual mentor through the years. In addition, all of my wonderful friends from my church were overlooked as well. The wedding plans continued.

On the day before the wedding, which happened to be my birthday, I became very ill. Steadily as the day wore on, my spring cold developed into a case of the flu; oh, I was so very sick.

Rosie came over to the house to take care of me. She sat by my bedside for hours late into the night, offering consolation and cheerful conversation as well as medical care. Rosie confided to me at this time that one of my daughters said Doc lies. My only defense was, "Don't we all at times."

The truth was, Doc had a manner of exaggerating many things. It was his way to try to present himself in an acceptable light to my family and others. This should not have been necessary as he was so likable. His seemingly self-assured manner was in place in spite of his suffering from deep insecurity.

In the meantime, my nose was running nonstop, my temperature was rising, and I was just miserable.

The only doctor I could locate on call on this Saturday evening was a total stranger to me. When I explained my predicament and that I would be getting married in the morning, he gave me a lot of sincere and sweet sympathy. My pathetic plea to this physician was for a wave of his wand for an instant, miraculous cure.

In the morning I remained in sorry condition. Nevertheless, the wheels were spinning, and the wedding would take place as planned. Already, the principals involved were beginning to step into their particular roles.

Susan and Doc drove over to Wolfie's Bakery on Sunrise Blvd. for the cake we had ordered. The cake was three-tiered and beautiful with the traditional bride-and-groom figure on the top. While bringing the cake home, Doc drove very slowly as Susan held the cake precariously on her lap. Just once, at a railroad crossing, the cake came dangerously close to being knocked over, creating a tense moment for Susan.

As the reception was to be held at the house, we began setting up for the expected guests.

Doc had begun to grow a beard which was quite sparse and wispy. Susan asked in a charming fashion that he shave it off. He told her he would, but it would be up to her "mama" to decide. Because I loved it as well as his sideburns and mustache, I wouldn't consider the request.

Meanwhile, no one seemed to realize just how wretched I felt. Flu symptoms were coursing through my body, producing coughing, sweating, and a runny nose. It seemed no one cared.

Soon, the house was ready for the reception, this same place that had hosted so many family celebrations through the years. This occasion today was due to what I had considered to be an impossible event. My wedding day! Here I was about to eat my famous last words, namely, "I'll never marry again."

My wedding dress was beige with sleeves that were fitted to the elbows and then a great flare and trimmed with lace. The neckline was low with a fitted bodice tied with laces from the waistline up. Down the center front from the waistline to the floor-length hemline were tiny red rosebuds. It was rather old fashioned and very lovely. The head piece, also beige, was composed of two flowers fashioned from stiff voile with netting extending over the eyes. As a matter of fact, the salesperson who helped me with this selection insisted anything more would be inappropriate "under the circumstances." All these subtle innuendos were undermining my already firmly established insecurities. I encouraged myself, silently: After all, wasn't marriage a sacred institution, highly regarded in our culture?

On this day it was not difficult to appreciate Doc's Adonis image. His wedding suit was blue-gray. The jacket had flaps and accented pockets. The vest and navy blue shirt and a monogrammed white tie completed the outfit, which was complemented by a white carnation in the lapel.

Our honor attendants – Gerry and Al – and Susan and Larry and Howard and Rosie followed us to the church.

We arrived at the church and waited inside for the Reverend Hutton. It was after 1:00 p.m. and the reverend was late. After all, it was Sunday, and he had already put in a full morning in church.

The reverend came dashing in ten minutes late, with an apology. As we proceeded with the ceremony, the very beautiful words flowed. The service was built on and filled with God's word addressing the issue of marriage.

Doc was visibly nervous and had trouble getting the ring on my finger. But he did not have a problem with the kiss that followed. Gerry cried tears of joy and then laughed with pleasure. Susan and Larry's presence was special to me.

Rosie elected to be the official photographer and took a series of pictures. The reverend was busy signing the marriage certificate. The mood was lighthearted as we left the church. Rosie and Howard were honking out "Here Comes the Bride" on their car horn as we drove over the bridge to the house, located directly across the river.

Thus far the seed bed has been planted with seed pearls, small and imperfect, seedlings in the seed bed which is a source of growth and gradual manifestation.

Chapter Six

An hour earlier I had left my house as a widow and upon my re-entry, my status had been drastically changed. In addition to the wedding party, friends and relatives had gathered to celebrate the wedding and to congratulate Mr. and Mrs. James Addison Foxx III.

On hand were the DeLeo's, Ed and Verdi; Gerry's sister Dot and her husband, Don; and my lovely friend Rita, a secretary from the college who was also a belly dancer. Rita, who had shared in the excitement of my courtship with Doc, was present with her lovely daughter. My daughter Kris with her beautiful little daughter, Laurie, was present as well. My daughter who was in Georgia sent a lovely bouquet of flowers. Dina was my "flower girl." The fact that my oldest brother, Jules, was in the area and able to be a part of this celebration was grand. Also, my oldest sister "B" with her husband, re-tired Lt. Col. Harrison Hogan, as well as my Aunt Lydia, her granddaughter Marion with her husband, Fred, and their son and daughter were on hand. Aunt Gladys, an aunt by mar-riage, now residing in Ft. Lauderdale, was present as well. She loved all my family and idolized Doc.

Ruth and Joe Madison, an elderly couple who lived down the street, joined in the festivities. "Ruthie" had been my neighborhood confidant and had admonished me to be careful in my romance. She secretly adored Doc and really took great pleasure in vicariously sharing my happiness and romantic escapades.

The mood was high. Doc was showing off the com-puterized watch I had given him. My brother Jules seemed fascinated with Doc's personality and at one point, as he was laughing at a comment of Doc's, Jules asked how old he was,

Doc replied, "Old enough to sleep alone, but I don't."

As we opened the gifts, "Grampa Doc" held the beautiful blonde Laurie in his arms. The fanfare began with ribbons and wrappings, followed by many "oohs" and "aahs" and other expressions of appreciation.

As Doc circulated among the guests, he continued to boastfully and proudly display the watch I had given him.

In the meantime, Jules had taken my friend Verdi out to the car to get his gift. Jules asked Verdi her opinion of a huge, magnificent, one hundred-year-old Bible he had for us. "Do you think they will like it?" he asked. Verdi replied, "It is perfect." Jules then said, "I knew I was keeping this for a very special occasion."

Doc was crazy about the Bible. He truly loved it as it represented beauty and knowledge. Pictures were taken of the presentation of the Bible.

The cake-cutting ceremony and champagne toasts were joyous. However, there was a point when I felt all alone. It was as though everyone had melted into the sidelines, and I was standing alone in the center of the house.

By contrast, my brother Jules was ecstatic. Jules was a high I.Q. personality and very charming. As Jules conveyed his feelings of joy for me, I said, "No matter what happens, I would not have missed this experience for the world."

Even though I was still feeling the effects of the flu with my nose dripping, the merrymaking continued. It all tapered off with the throwing of the bouquet, which Aunt Gladys caught! The guests began to take their leave. Soon, Doc and I were alone. I changed into my traveling outfit.

Doc asked, "Are you happy we're married?"

Still not feeling too great, I said, "Oh, I don't know, are you?"

He replied, "Shoot, yeah, I've never been happier."

It was apparent to me that he couldn't understand my attitude.

We had plane reservations for Chattanooga, Tennessee. This had been my idea, in part because I knew Doc loved this part of the country and also because I'd never really visited this area.

Feeling as I was, I suggested we postpone the trip. However, we did not. It seemed the right thing to do since all the arrangements had been made.

Actually, it was a lot of fun in spite of my lingering flu symptoms. At the airport we observed the security measures. As Doc walked through the scanner, the bells clanged with fury, and he was frisked!

Although everyone attempted to act serious, Doc looked so adorable that people laughed. Deep down, I was proud of my handsome husband. And he did lavish attention on me. His attentiveness to me was the kind women appreciate, and it was so nice. Not only had I begun to take this attentiveness for granted, I absorbed it.

The spirit of the day continued. Once on the plane, as the personnel realized we were honeymooners, we were given drinks and offered congratulatory toasts. Also, a flight attendant gave us an extra souvenir bottle of whiskey. She confided that she was not supposed to do this, but "under the circumstances," she couldn't resist.

The flight was beautiful, and once we landed, we proceeded to rent a car, using my Visa card. Doc said he'd make it all up and that I could have the settlement he anticipated receiving when we got back. He was truly concerned about this, but it somehow did not worry me in the least.

The car we rented was big and black and shiny with importance. We immediately headed for a diner Doc had promised to take me to. This was a diner that reportedly had hosted Elvis Presley. Nevertheless, the diner was noted for its catfish and proved worthy of its fame. I was convinced that Doc was indeed acquainted with this area and knew whereof he spoke.

Later (it was after midnight by then), we checked into a Holiday Inn. Once in the room, still fighting my symptoms, I began nursing my condition, and television was high on Doc's agenda. He was avoiding my illness.

After breakfast the next morning, we went shopping. We bought matching orange T-shirts which read "Tennessee" and, in white, the number 55. As we walked and window shopped, I found Chattanooga to be a most interesting place. The song "Chattanooga Choo Choo" started running through my mind.

Doc was looking around for his "daddy." I strongly suggested that he make every possible effort to see his father. We then walked to a bar known as "Jimmy's." Doc seemed to feel his father might possibly be there.

"There might be some girls who work here that will show me a lot of affection, but don't get upset as they are like stepsisters to me," Doc said. However, at the time, I did not feel threatened by such an encounter. Actually, I felt it extremely important for Doc to see his "daddy." "Daddy" seemed to be a distant person and a father who had not been especially available to his son.

Jimmy's bar was rather deserted, with only the bar attendant on hand. It was a small place with a few pool tables and the bar. The attendant knew Doc and said his father hadn't been around for a while. Doc then mentioned a hotel as a possible place he might locate his father. I said, "Let's go."

The hotel was in the same vicinity, and we walked to this giant stone building which appeared to be more of a rooming house than a hotel. After checking with no results, Doc decided to give up seeking his daddy for the time being.

As we descended the wide, stone stairway to the street, a man called to Doc. The person came closer and said he wanted to talk to Doc privately. Doc said, "Go ahead. You can say whatever you have to in front of her. She is my wife." But the guy insisted on speaking to Doc alone.

"It's all right," I said. "Go on and talk to him alone."

Actually it didn't bother me or mean anything to me at that moment. However, I noted the person was rather short of stature. He was wearing a gray outfit, matching pants and shirt widely sold as work clothes. In addition, I noticed his hair was dark, rather long and unruly. He could not be classified as neat. This person, a stranger to me, and Doc walked several feet away and exchanged words for a few minutes. And then, as Doc started walking toward me, I heard the person say, "I'm telling you, get out of town or you will be shot." Doc did not appear to be perturbed by this. I was thinking it was weird and there must be odd people in this city. And then I put the incident completely out of my mind.

Look Out Mountain on Prestige Hill was a place Doc was excited about showing me. As we rode up this mountain, I felt a sense of the true greatness of God and a deep appreciation of the terrain.

Later that same day we left Tennessee and drove into Georgia. The first stop was a visit to an uncle who lived in a small mobile home, one of three on this miniature family mobile-home compound. One of these was the home of Granny's sister Lena, who bore a remarkable resemblance to Granny. The compound contained various "kin." The location was behind a small store on a bit of a hill.

It amused me no end when I realized (after meeting these folks) that it was suspected we were gangsters or something of the sort due to the big black rental car and the fact that we were well dressed. One of the uncles hid until we were identified. Actually, this peculiar scenario began to seem normal to me in this environment, and I did not view their behavior as bizarre.

After a brief visit at the family compound, we drove to a rural residential area in this same vicinity to visit yet another cousin. In this instance I was truly impressed as there were very young children who obviously recognized and loved Doc. Even though these little ones had not seen Doc for a long time, they were at ease with him, and he enjoyed them. Doc had charisma with children as well as a partiality for youngsters.

While visiting here, Doc's cousin told him that she saw his father occasionally. She then suggested that if we were to write to Doc's father in care of her address, she would see to it that he would get the letter. This mysterious father person! How could one relate to this illusive father figure?

After this visit we headed for Ruby Falls. Although I was still sniffing and suffering mildly, I tried to be a good sport. The experience of the Falls appealed to me and my interest in history. If I felt better than I did that day, I would have enjoyed it tremendously.

Before we embarked on the tour inside the mountain, which began with an elevator ride, Doc bought me a blue beaded bag. As we proceeded to the trail, marching along with many other tourists, Doc was joking and had the folks around us laughing. All this should have been much fun for me, however, halfway through the procession I said, "Let's go back, I'm just not up to this." Doc agreed.

Back in the big black car, we drove to Granny's. As we drove into Granny's yard, the feeling of excitement that Doc's presence generated was evident as the children ran inside to announce our arrival. Once inside, we were soon engaged in conversation, Doc with his cousins, and I with Granny. Granny expressed her pleasure concerning our marriage. She then said, "James has a good woman."

We were offered a sampling of "soul food" simmering in a big pot on the kitchen stove. Following this we prepared to leave. Once in the car, one of the children asked Doc if they could have some money. The child said it had been requested by the adults inside.

As we drove off, I realized there was deep within me, a special, nameless affinity to these people and to this Georgia culture so different from my own.

When we arrived at the airport in Atlanta, the thoughts and feelings of my pensive mood shifted in anticipation of the plane ride back to Ft. Lauderdale.

PART II: THE PROPAGATION OF THE SEED BED

Chapter Seven

The state of being married seemed profound in its simplicity. Doc's demeanor was constant with his ever-cheerful morning greetings, his thoughtfulness in little things, and his ever-present sense of and joy in silly fun.

Also, the "surprises," both small and big gifts of love, continued. Anything that pleased me seemed to be his personal pleasure. He said it was all worthwhile "just to see the look on your face." I was "his woman," to be cherished.

Sometimes an undercurrent of tension would manifest within me which I found difficult to release. It was at these times Doc would use his marvelous talent for massaging to relax me. His wonderful hands would work dexterously over my body, easing every muscle with the expertise of a professional masseuse. Ultimately, the completion culminated in our spirits intertwining as one.

This oneness rolled as on the crest of an ocean wave, utterly delightful in the exhilaration of our union. Tossing and rolling and weaving, and then peaking, resulted in the inevitable crescendo and crash on the shore.

Being Doc's woman had many pluses, and my thoughts seemed to return to the words my oldest daughter had penned in high school:

"Beneath my feet is lush green grass
and in my hand a flower –
But wait; what is this?

I am pushing ahead and upward
through green tree tops, past snow
capped mountains . . . looking forward
to and beyond the blue sky, the
white fluffy clouds.
Beyond this – dark night, weightlessness.
And yet I push farther ahead, on to cold,
yet fiery, diamonds called stars.
This is expected of me, for I am Youth.
But what of the things I have left
behind? The reassuring firmness
beneath my feet, the loveliness I held
in my hand? I shall have both! The
thrill of conquest shall go hand in hand
with peace and serenity.
I shall have both, for I am Youth."

Although surrounded by the poetry of life, I nevertheless found my own imagination waning in the true art of living. It became only a matter of time before my programmed
"nine-to-five" theory of how to live began to surface.

Gently, the inner nagging began. Surely it was time
for Doc to get settled in a job. Doc agreed. However, I was ill
prepared for the incredible series of events that would follow.

Since carpet installation seemed to be the most interesting possibility in the labor market for Doc, we concentrated
on seeking opportunity in this area of employment. In answer

to an ad in the paper, we eagerly set out to do an assignment for an independent business person located in Hollywood. I found myself as an assistant to Doc, using my Firebird as a vehicle to pick up, deliver, and then help to install the carpet as well.

For me, all this was fun. Doc did all the heavy work, which he seemed to thrive on, and my part was mostly as an observer.

When the work had been accomplished and it was time to be paid, we went to the employer's apartment. This person lived in a small, somewhat sleazy apartment complex. We knocked on the door, and it was opened partially, as far as the chain link would allow. When the employer saw who it was, he flatly refused to pay and then closed the door. Incredible!

Although I was aware the left side of my brain is dormant concerning business matters, I was, nonetheless, shocked. What happened to the verbal agreement in this business deal? Also, what about the investment of time, labor, and the expenses involved? Were they all for naught? Apparently so. There was nothing one could do concerning this situation to recover the dollars and cents lost that would be worth the trouble.

The next venture of employment for Doc was a position on the midnight shift with Broward General Hospital. It seemed ideal since Doc had a flair for this type of work due to his medical knowledge. Doc looked handsome in the white uniform he wore for the job, and he enjoyed the status it provided.

But the midnight shift! This annoyed me. I felt that not only was the pay scale unfair at minimum wage, but I also felt I did not get married to spend my nights alone.

Therefore, Doc called his supervisor and told her

I was paranoid about spending my nights alone. As I was listening to this conversation on the extension as Doc had asked me to do, I got the distinct impression that she really liked Doc a lot. The tiny hearts and flowers were in her understanding voice as she spoke to him. He, however, did not seem to notice, and he did want to keep the job. The supervisor agreed to have him work on the day shift.

My cousin Marion, a nurse at the hospital, told me that Doc worked so well with the patients in the psychiatric ward, especially with the younger children. Evidently he managed to get the patients to cooperate with him in ways that were important such as eating, etc., and helped them to find a measure of enjoyment in doing so.

One day Doc came home with a lovely white beaded choker embellished with a green center made by a patient for me. The patients also wrote loving statements to Doc.

Shortly after Doc began this position with the hospital, my oldest brother, Jules, and his friend Rosie drove over from the west coast of Florida to visit. We made plans to have lunch with Doc at the hospital.

We arrived at the hospital at the designated time and spotted Doc walking in the corridor. As we walked up behind him, I noticed that Doc nodded a greeting to a nurse. Based on this observation I said to Doc in a barely audible voice, "I'm going to divorce you." The blood literally drained from his face, and Doc turned chalk white. He couldn't understand my statement and, incredibly, neither could I! The lunch period that followed was a strain.

Later, I used the fact that the pay Doc received was quite meagerto convince Doc to quit his job.

Chapter Eight

In the meantime, the perpetual diet to maintain beauty, of course, remained ever present. This first summer of my marriage found me visting a doctor's office, actually a doctor I never really met.

The trip to this office was a weekly event. A nurse or receptionist issued packets of flavored powder which was to be blended with skim milk or water. Naturally there was a choice of flavors. The six hundred calories a day supplied by this method was indeed a way to lose weight. It was also extremely expensive. As my weight decreased with this "nothing" method of dieting and my determination to have it so, something else began happening. I started to throw up quantities of yellow bile.

When I phoned the doctor's office and asked to speak to the doctor, a nurse took the information and cheerfully said the yellow bile was nothing to worry about.

A week later, Susan and Larry and Doc and I spent the afternoon at Whiskey Creek. The day was gorgeous, and the sun very hot. This beach party was very relaxing, and I was obsessed with soaking up the sunshine. Previous to leaving the beach, I realized all the drinks were gone, and I had neglected to have any. After we left the beach, we all decided to go to the New England Oyster House for dinner. Susan planned to borrow some clothes of mine to wear in order to save a trip back to her apartment in Plantation.

Once at home, as I began to dress, a feeling of dizziness swept over me. I said, "I don't feel well but I'm sure I'll be okay in a few minutes." I then excused myself and laid down on the bed. My eyeballs began flipping around like a TV set spinning out of whack. At least that was the sensation

I experienced. Whoa! What was happening here? The next thing I knew Doc had me in his arms and carried me to the car. He placed me across the back seat and laid my head on a bed pillow.

A wild ride to the hospital followed. It was difficult to determine which was worse, the ride or the illness. A siren surely would have been in order to complete the scenario.

After a week in the hospital and many tests, including nuclear medicine, a decision to release me was made. The personnel and staff gave me no advice, no medicine, and no explanation. This had, indeed, been an experience in futility.

Nevertheless, I believed I had suffered some degree of dehydration and the medical personnel in attendance at the hospital had, in my person, a terrific guinea pig.

In the interim, Doc obtained another carpet job. The job was with a salesman, an Englishman, who was employed by a large carpet firm. This person possessed much charm and wit, which were enhanced by his accent.

The job assignment proved to be another disappointment. In complying with the instructions we soon found ourselves at an apartment complex which proved small and crowded. Next, we were to switch a carpet (used and very worn out) to another apartment within the complex. New sections of carpet were to be pieced and added as necessary. Also, we noticed the resident of this apartment had nine cats. At this point Doc phoned the salesman to inform him of the many problems encountered on this project. The convincing voice with the English accent was smooth and reassuring. He owed the apartment manager a favor, he said. "Go ahead with it," he said. "It should be fine."

However, the whole operation proved, at best, a disaster. This entire deal was a crude arrangement that left much to be desired.

When the time came to collect the five-hundred-dollar fee, the formerly charming voice with the English accent became indignant and flatly refused to pay.

Nevertheless, we managed to collect a third of the amount owed. A detective friend of ours, appalled by the situation, made a series of veiled threats via telephone to the English carpet salesman. In turn, this person paid us, as he was obviously frightened of the possible repercussions noted in the threats.

On a happier note, we had fun when we decided to purchase a pool table and to sell the den furniture to make room for the game table. To celebrate this decision, we promptly decided to have an impromptu chili, pool, and poker party. Our amazed guests, who were all family, came in spite of the short notice, perhaps out of curiosity. All three of my daughters and their husbands came, and the event proved very enjoyable.

We all played pool, and then the guys played poker. My oldest daughter's husband, a champion at the game of tennis, was also very good at the game of poker. Doc came to me once or twice during the poker game, trying to explain something that was troubling him. Apparently it had something to do with the fact that he did not hold the winning hand. In any event, I really did not understand the game. In spite of this, the overall pleasure of the evening was enhanced by a crock pot filled with delicious chili, served with lots of garlic bread.

Chapter Nine

As time went on, the attorney for Doc's continuing lawsuit was becoming more difficult to contact. We now had all the necessary evidence, as well as witnesses to the incident that took place in Guantanamo Bay, Cuba, when Doc was injured.

Sometime later we learned why there was difficulty in our communication efforts. It seems the attorney in question had a personal life crisis, that is, a divorce, and a subsequent new bride. Apparently this had caused a breech in the continuity of his business affairs.

In the meantime, Doc had connected with yet another job. The job was mainly to drive an employer's truck in this man's own new business venture. It also included transporting loads of dirt from, literally, sunup till sundown. Doc did this assignment faithfully for three weeks.

When a pay check failed to materialize, I insisted that Doc demand one. The man finally wrote a check which equaled one week's salary. We took the check directly to the Coral Springs bank on which it was written. The cashier hesitated to cash the check as the account was in a dubious state. Fortunately, however, she did honor it.

In yet another instance, a job with a well known Ft. Lauderdale roofing company proved to be still another disastrous affair. Doc was hired to shingle roofs in a large housing development in the northeast section of this growing city.

For one entire week, he shingled roofs. Also, in order to meet a deadline for the company, Doc worked right through the weekend. I worked with him and actually climbed on the roofs to assist him with the work. There was no one in sight; no company personnel in charge of this operation were to be seen anywhere on the premises. It seemed strange to me.

Doc went to the company office on the designated pay day to receive his wages and was told to get off the premises or they would call the police.

As a result, Doc was very confused and upset. We later contacted the police from our home. Their reply was that the company was within their rights to order anyone off the property, and we simply had no recourse.

The events on the job front were incredible. If I had not been closely and personally involved in these situations, I would find it all difficult to believe. It was indeed small comfort to realize this kind of activity was prevalent at this time in the South Florida area. Concurrently, I heard many people calling in to radio talk shows and expressing similar dilemmas in their own personal encounters with the labor market.

Chapter Ten

About this point in time, Susan and Larry were making plans to build a home in Palm Hills, a suburban area located west of West Palm Beach in Florida. This vicinity presented a country atmosphere with narrow, winding, paved roads, bridle paths and many canals bordering the properties.

"Country Boy" Doc and I decided to purchase five beautiful acres which were just two miles by land or water from Susan.

After we acquired this home site, our dreams began to take form via happy plans.

On a whim one day, we decided to visit our property. It was suggested we stay at the Holiday Inn in Belle Glade. Unfortunately, we realized too late there was a much more convenient place to stay which was the Inn at Grand Floral Beach.

After all was said and done, we had checked in at the Inn in Belle Glade on a Friday evening and the next morning drove to Palm Hills.

As we drove through this area of lovely trees and the winding roads my heart sang "over the river and through the woods, to grandmother's house we go."

Actually, we were as two little kids as we checked out our treasure of land. The five acres bordered by a canal seemed enormous. Across the canal one could see cows grazing contentedly. I was especially intrigued by a giant petrified tree on our land.

After spending some time here exchanging and expanding our dream thoughts to each other, we decided to check on Susan's property. Two miles and two bridges around the bend and we were there.

Upon our arrival we discovered a sign posted on a tree on the property indicating the construction phase of their house was scheduled to begin soon. We were elated at the prospect of relating this news to Susan and Larry.

As we explored further, we made comparisons to our property. This virgin area was beautiful with much to build on and much to do.

The Firebird was parked near the entrance to the property, and, since there was no driveway developed as yet, we were parked on a sandy spot.

When we tried to leave, the car became stuck in the sand. I got out of the car and as Doc attempted to move the car, the tires became deeply enmeshed in the sand. Doc tried placing stones and loose wood under the tires. Nothing worked. Doc then raced the motor, and the wheels kept spinning and grinding more deeply into the sand.

As I gently suggested it might be best to stop the motor, Doc became furious. At that moment it seemed all the frustrations of his lifetime culminated and a maniacal monster emerged. Doc jumped out of the car and began pounding me. I started to run. Oh, dear God, there was no place to run to. Screaming and calling for help was in vain as the place was deserted. Oh, God, this is insane! I ran a distance and got behind a small tree. This, of course, was useless as he grabbed me and beat on me, and, as he tossed me about, I had an inner vision of my being as defenseless as a rag doll. Even in those terrifying moments I sensed he was venting all the accumulated disappointments he had suffered during his growing-up years. I was, in the face of this situation, helpless.

After the horror of this scene was over, we walked a good distance before we found a telephone. Finally, help arrived, and the car was rescued from the sand.

We returned to the motel and Doc's remorse and shame over the incident was apparent. On the other hand, my feelings and thoughts were in utter confusion as I tended to my bruises.

Despite his remorsefulness, my state of mind, coupled with disillusionment, did not prevent me from telling Doc this sort of thing had better never happen again.

It took time for our very different moods to change. And ugh! The motel room carpet was quite soaked due to a leak in the building. The wet carpet just seemed to emphasize the already revolting atmosphere that dominated this oppressive situation.

Chapter Eleven

We returned home and as the summer wore on, the correspondence with Doc's attorney became more frequent. We had produced evidence and also witnesses to the alleged incident which were finally acknowledged and taken under consideration.

The tempo of our lives changed, and we marched to the tune of different jobs, as well as frequent visits to doctor's offices which were necessary to satisfy requirements of the impending lawsuit. Also the approaching holidays helped as love once again became the nucleus around which the events of our lives seem to spin and without which we could not have survived.

Throughout our daily experience, the winds of change were ever so gently set in motion. The course and direction of our life together began to shift. Doc had learned of a possibility for work with a large West Palm Beach construction firm. He became determined to seek work in this location. I accompanied Doc to this site and spent an entire day waiting around for Doc to be hired and he was, eventually. Although the whole spectrum of this particular job situation seemed shady to me (just a feeling due to the way personnel handled the hiring), I bowed humbly in the face of Doc's obvious pleasure at being hired. The high wage promised and expected was quickly reduced to minimum wage.

A minor change in my life style came when I found myself driving to West Palm Beach with Doc on a daily basis. This proved to be a long haul and kept me away from Ft. Lauderdale a great deal of the time.

The next change was a major one, as we decided to move to West Palm Beach. Little did I realize that the first

Christmas of my marriage would prove to be the very last Christmas I would spend in my Ft. Lauderdale home.

We moved soon after the holidays. We found a lovely apartment in the village of Royal Palm Beach. The apartment was located near a canal and only several miles from Palm Hills. It wasn't long before another change occurred. My intuitive feelings concerning Doc's job had proved accurate.

Doc then took a job with the county water department. This, at the time, seemed it might conceivably prove to be a worthwhile opportunity as Doc attended a college class sponsored by the department in order to become certified for the job. Although Doc seemed to like this job, it was not long before he separated from this position. In the meantime, the seeming futility of this whole situation began to spell out a message for me.

It was at this point I decided to seek employment. Upon my first interview, I obtained a position as a counselor in a battered- women's program.

After my interview, Doc met me at Jefferson's restaurant on Okeechobee Boulevard. He said he was so proud of me as he presented me with a congratulatory gift.

The gift was a lovely silver chain, which was in a blue box wrapped with a white ribbon. Doc had pawned his cherished 350 magnum at Dick and Harry's, a pawn shop, for $30.00 in order to buy the gift.

Once again Doc was seeking work and found employment with another large construction firm. The job did, in fact, pay a better wage. Also, the lawsuit was settled for $2,000.00

We sought out living quarters in the city of West Palm Beach and located a really interesting apartment in the Viking Wings complex. The building faced the Intracoastal Waterway and was located just a few blocks from my office.

My job was most interesting, as helping women in distress was most rewarding. Doc was always helpful and cooperative to the point that I reminded him that I could, indeed, handle my own work. However, some of the situations I found myself involved in as the result of my work had a certain potential for danger, especially the weekend assignments on beeper call. In addition, I began to develop anxiety symptoms due to a rather incompatible relationship at work.

All the same, in essence, life was full and interesting. Palm Beach was just "over the bridge." This is a rich and beautiful area and the distinctive aspect of this atmosphere had its influence in the way we lived and moved.

In the meantime, Doc and I found a restaurant downtown that could be considered a "hole in the wall." It became our secret place. This place served a variety of vegetables, ten at least, at low prices. The clientele consisted of variety of people, from the downtown derelict to the more noteworthy business person. And my beeper never failed to call me before I completed a meal here.

Also, about this time we became involved in taking disco dance lessons as the Saturday Night Fever rage was sweeping the country. Doc felt his masculinity was being threatened as he had to become a Y.W.C.A. member in order to take the lessons being offered here. Actually, it was just a required card, and we enjoyed the dancing.

My symptoms of anxiety were becoming quite pronounced, especially in the middle of the night when I would awaken from a sound sleep and have to leave the apartment. It was then we decided the "inside apartment" was contributing to my condition.

I began using a technique which was new to me. In meditation I developed an image of my desire as I pictured the place I would like to live.

Within a few days we were moving to an apartment on Dixie Highway. This apartment was on the top floor and every room had a view that over looked the Intracoastal Waterway. It was delightful. Moving was easy for me as Doc cheerfully took over all the heavy work. Actually, he had great manners, an attribute that southeners often seem to have.

The new neighborhood was interesting, as many of the West Palm Beach's areas are. We quickly adapted to our new surroundings. I resigned my position, for it was the best solution to the situation that had developed within the office. When the clients recognized and began to remark about the treatment I was receiving, it was time to leave.

Chapter Twelve

In the fall of 1978 I was hired by the public school system. The credit hours I had accumulated in my college experience were sufficient for me to qualify for a part-time position. It was great. I "floated" and served in classrooms and/or the office where help was needed.

In the meantime, Doc secured a job with a carpet firm located a few blocks from where we lived. Once again, he was assigned jobs that were offbeat. At one point Doc had asked me to pick up a check for him. When I met the person in charge, he appeared to have a sick stomach. It was just a look that made me draw this conclusion. He was a bit rude to me and when I told him I worked for the school board, a sickening expression crossed his pale face as he said in a voice filled with disbelief, "You work for the school system?"

This same person suggested that Doc take the truck home for the night so that he could drive directly to his next day's assignment. This went on for two evenings. Doc parked the truck and did not use it until the morning. However, this man with the sick look eventually tried to accuse Doc of stealing the truck.

These events led up to a fateful morning in November. I had gone to work as usual and was on the job just two hours when I was called to the office. There was a young black man with a message for me. I recognized him as a person who was helping Doc on his job. He had ridden his bicycle to the school. The message was that Doc had purchased two tickets and was at the airport. His destination was Georgia. This was shocking to me.

Why? Why was this happening? According to the message, by the time I received it Doc was already gone.

Perhaps I was expected to rush to the airport. It was too late. I was very upset. I went to the apartment and found all of his things were gone. I don't remember what I did the rest of the day. I may have called Larry, for later in the day Larry and Susan came to my apartment. I remember having a bad headache and an upset stomach.

I continued with my job. I especially recall the cook in the cafeteria who was always so nice to me. In my shocked state of mind she talked to me and was a friend. This same person made sure I ate a good meal at noon time. In the meantime, the person at the carpet company with the sick look began calling me up and rattled on, speaking to me in a strange way, questioning me and insinuating many things. I listened only because I thought he might reveal something I should know. However, I was advised not to converse with him.

At one point he mentioned that he came from a southern "aristocratic" family. When I told my friend the cook at school, she stated, "That's the worst kind." It was obvious that there was something shady this man was involved in as he had an incredible amount of information that was not confined to just a lowly carpet employee, as Doc certainly was. Something sinister was in the air.

Communication was started via phone calls. Doc was at his mother's home in Georgia. From conversations with his mother I gathered that he was working on construction jobs. Upon his arrival she said he had appeared with no luggage as he had hitchhiked from Atlanta and left his luggage by the side of the road, later retrieving it. Evidently he was experiencing a measure of contentment in this environment. I didn't know what to do. I went to see an attorney for advice and received little.

Doc began calling me on the phone and reversing

the charges. (The phone was in his name.) He asked me to come to Georgia to live, stating we could rent a mobile home. Something inside me held me back. Within, there was a feeling that caused me to resist that I can only describe as a steel rod. It was an ever-present force. What was this strong feeling? Why? Why couldn't I go? This was a person who had made the stars seem so bright for me. A person that had made me come alive, and now I could not respond to. Why? What was this force within me that prevented me from running to the person I once thought could move the planet?

It was nearing Thanksgiving Day, and Doc asked me to come to Georgia for the holiday. Because he pleaded sincerely, I said I might. On Thanksgiving Day my daughter Kris and her family came to my apartment as we were all going to Susan and Larry's. Doc called and said, "You're not coming are you?" He was disappointed. The steel rod held me firm. We talked for at least an hour. He spoke to Kris and then we said goodbye.

After the holidays I realized my living expenses could not be managed on my part-time pay. Therefore, I sought a full-time position with the school system. The person who interviewed me was extremely understanding of my problems and immediately placed me in a position assisting foreign students. It was a Godsend for many reasons. The same woman who gave me this opportunity was my supervisor. The teacher whom I assisted, Mike Tass, and also Martha Taylor, an assistant, were delightful to work with. In spite of my personal misfortune, the job was a special charm to me. The students were so interesting, and the work proved most rewarding.

As the Christmas holidays approached, Doc's phone calls increased. The calls were all collect, and the phone bill mounted. One evening I received a call from an operator for the phone company. It was concerning payment of the bill. As I explained my situation, the person I spoke with was very sympathetic and concerned for me. Although I told her where Doc could be reached as the bill was in his name, and also requested the phone be disconnected, this kind person said I shouldn't be without a phone during the holidays as I was alone.

After the holidays, on a Saturday in January, Doc appeared suddenly and without warning. I felt strange and frightened. He said he knew I didn't want to "sleep" with him and asked me if I'd received the insurance check, the settlement for the Cuban incident. I said I had and that the money was used for attorney fees and doctor bills. The air was strained, and I said I was going to a movie. Doc stayed close and followed along. We went to a theater on Palm Beach Lakes Boulevard. I kept thinking that on the pretext of using the ladies room, I might quietly slip away. However, Doc must have sensed my intention as he watched me closely.

We returned to the apartment, at which point I suggested talking to the police. My purpose was to seek advice and/or help. I felt desperate. On the other hand, Doc, as soon as I mentioned police said, "No, no police," and wasted no time in leaving. I don't believe his plans included leaving in this way as he left some prescription medication and other items on the table.

Gone again! I had no idea how he traveled, whether by car, plane, train, bus, or thumb. Once again I felt confused and as an exile within my own person.

Why could I have not just talked and tried to make sense out of the chaos of this situation? Being abandoned had filled me with doubt and anxiety. I was wary and unable to trust. I was evidently left helpless to communicate in a situation that my subconscious dictated as hopeless.

Today and tomorrow were days to exist and endure.

Solution solving had not yet appeared on the daily menu. The propagation of the seed bed was as if moving through a medium.

PART III: TARES

Chapter Thirteen

Alone again, naturally. As I went over in my mind the last encounter I had with Doc, I could not resolve the futility of it all. The "why" of it was impossible to determine. In the meantime, having a job to concentrate on was a saving grace.

One evening, my sister Florence and her husband, Frank, came to my apartment for dinner. This was an event I scheduled in order to ensure life in as normal a fashion as possible, as well as to fill an unexplainable void.

The occasion was a success and most enjoyable as Flo and I talked about our growing-up years in Connecticut. Flo always had the marvelous facility of remembering names and events that I had long forgotten. It proved to be a great escape mechanism for me. I served apple pie and ice cream for dessert, and my guests had brought a huge Carvel pie. It seemed we were destined and determined to finish as much of this tempting crowning to a delicious meal as we possibly could.

Around midnight I invited them to stay the night. Somehow, internally, it was extremely important to me. However, they politely declined and left. Alone again in my empty apartment, I put the dishes away and retired. I woke very early the next morning and was aware of a dull, aching throb in the middle of my forehead. It must be due to eating an overabundance of the unaccustomed desserts at dinner, I thought. In my mind I was wondering what to do about Doc's mail that had accumulated. He had called and said he would be returning. Nevertheless, I was not sure as to what I should do. As the dull ache continued, these thoughts were turning round in my head. And, on this Sunday morning, at precisely 6:00 a.m., I realized someone was knocking at my door.

I walked to the door and called out, "Who's there?"
The answer came back, "It's the police, I have an urgent message for you." I went to a window where I could see that, indeed, it was a policeman. I quickly opened the door, and the officer handed me a phone number which he said I needed to call right away.

I was anxious about the area code as my three daughters were living in three different cities, and it could be any one of them. Strangely, I did not think of Doc. Then I began to focus. The area code was 404 and that meant Georgia, where Doc was located.

Many thoughts ran through my mind. Was he in trouble? What was I to do? If he needed me, I thought, then I would surely go and help. Wait and see.

I drove to a phone booth. The booth was located on the corner of Broadway, a few blocks from my apartment. I dialed the number and asked for Sgt. Adelson, the name that was on the message. Sgt. Adelson had a most kindly manner. He began asking me a few questions concerning when I had seen Doc last and also how long Doc had been in Georgia.

I explained that Doc had left three months ago and had asked me via telephone to join him in Georgia. Also, I stated that I was thoroughly confused as I did not understand any of these actions. As a matter of fact, the entire happening and subsequent series of events confused me. I felt I could not join him for a number of reasons, including work, finances and health (it was important for me to live in a warm climate). I proceeded to tell Sgt. Adelson that I was totally perplexed and bewildered, especially since Doc had gone to his mother's home, as it would be the last place I would have expected him to be. Then Sgt. Adelson said, "I guess there is no other way to say it except that your husband passed away last night."

I replied, "Passed away? What do you mean? Was there an accident?"

Sgt. Adelson said, "Yes, it was an accident, he was shot." My grief and shock were beyond belief.

Sgt. Adelson then asked if my husband had ever mentioned the Klu Klux Klan. I replied that he had. Actually, it was when I first met him, but I didn't think much about it and it was soon forgotten.

Doc had talked about the Klan and having a "father figure." He had something written down in a little book and presumably there was to be some kind of meeting around the time he told me about it.

Doc had also mentioned that he had an "inherited" place in the organization due to his own father's membership. Doc also described the wearing apparel of the Klan and told me things that I thought could have been gleaned from movies or books. Furthermore, his relationship with his father was so distant that it seemed rather unlikely.

After that time, nothing more had ever been mentioned about this other than seeing a movie about the Klan that played at the Riverland Road drive-in theater. That was the extent of discussion of the Klan between us.

The next thing I became aware of was Sgt. Adelson saying, "Your husband was found in a pasture, executed gangland style, with his head blown off by a shot gun." He then told me he had spoken to Doc's mother at 5:00 a.m. that same morning, and when I asked how she was, he replied, "You are certainly taking the news harder than anyone else."

Then Sgt. Adelson went on to say that it might make me feel better to know that, according to a couple Doc visited frequently, Doc had often spoken about returning to me in Florida. I replied, "Of course, he had a good life here."

After this conversation, I was in total and absolute shock. The first place I called was my brother Bob's home in Boynton Beach. Bob and his wife said they would come to my apartment or that I should come there. Whatever was best for me, whatever I wished. My apartment. . .oh no! I couldn't face that.

Then I drove around aimlessly and found myself at a phone booth on Palm Beach Lakes Blvd. I phoned one of my daughters. It turned out that all three of them were together at her house. When I told Kris that Doc was dead, I was literally shouting. She asked how I knew and I shouted, "The police said his head was shot off!" Kris began to moan and scream. Then I spoke to Susan and Larry. I found myself wondering what to do about feeding their dogs as I had promised to do so while they were away.

Next I phoned my dear friends the DeLeo's in Ft. Lauderdale. I said, "Ed, I don't know what to do about anything." After I related the news Ed said, "You'll find a way to go to the funeral, for I've always known you to do the decent thing." My friends Gerry and Al in Ft. Lauderdale must be told as they were the honor attendants at our wedding. Another collect call.

I began to drive around and around. People in other cars began motioning to me as I was evidently driving in the wrong lane.

On Old Dixie Highway going north at the corner of Belvedere Road, there is an intersection that begins one-way traffic that I was facing. Cars came to a standstill. Faces in the cars were smiling at me as they were waiting for me to get out of the way. Someone called out, "You're in the wrong lane." I said, bewildered and confused, "How come?"

They had no way of knowing the state of shock and the numbness I was experiencing. Soon I was on the Interstate and then I found myself at a phone booth in Lake Worth in front of a motel. I was calling Bob's apartment again. He said he would come and get me, but I said no. Again I found myself driving south on the interstate.

It was at this point that I was determined to go to my brother's apartment. However, I realized I was well past the exit. "Oh God! Oh God! What am I doing?" Then I realized I must get to Bob's apartment as I was in a dangerous frame of mind.

Chapter Fourteen

In the meantime, members of my family had gathered at my brother's apartment to embrace me with their love and compassionate support.

My family did the things that one in shock does not immediately recognize, all the loving, thoughtful things that are poured from the cup of kindness and caring, the caring that embraces you in your need.

Someone suggested that I call Doc's mother. Oh, of course, I called. Doc's mother was so very kind. She was very gentle as we spoke, and I realized she thought I had not been informed of the brutality of the death. Doc's mother then asked me what I wanted to do about the funeral. My mind had still not even partially grasped the reality of the significance of this bizarre tragedy. I replied something about her doing what needed to be done as it was all "up there."

My brother Art advised me not to go. Naturally he was apprehensive under the circumstances. He felt anything involving gun play and also the mysterious events surrounding the death created a potentially dangerous situation.

However, my sister Flo and her husband Frank said I must go. It was the "Christian" thing to do. In addition, they graciously consented to go with me.

As the arrangements and decisions concerning the trip were being discussed, my mind seemed to be weaving through a muddled haze.

Susan and Larry cut short their trip and arrived so quickly with their love and concern. How important these connections become that we take so for granted in the normal course of living.

I called the teacher in charge of my program, and

hysterically announced the news of Doc's death. In his always kindly manner, he told me not to worry about work.

Chapter Fifteen

The next morning, Flo and Frank drove me to Kris's home in central Florida. The four-hour drive didn't register in my head. I was oblivious to time; suddenly, we were there. Kris said she would drive us to Georgia in her car. Also, Kris insisted on doing all the driving.

The drive to Georgia – was it a moment or many hours? My mind was not recording time.

Seated in front of Doc's closed casket that evening with his mother, I turned to her and said, "I would like to view Doc's body." Something deep inside me had awakened. This grotesque moment nudged my soul. His mother jumped up. She said it wouldn't be possible. Then I followed her as she immediately went to the owner of the funeral home.

The next thing I knew I was being ushered into a small sitting room. My daughter Kris had watched what was going on and followed us. Later I learned that Kris had barely managed to slip in as the door was being shut on her. In my state of mind, I was not aware of her anxiety for me and the fact that she was taking good care of me.

The owner began explaining that it was not possible for me to view the body. He said something about something being sealed.

Still bleary of mind, I guess I understood him to be saying that the casket was sealed. It was not until later I realized what he had said was they had to seal Doc's head. Nor did I know at this time I had a legal right to a viewing. Why then all this mystery? I just wanted to see a part of him, his hand or a tattoo. Kris also later stated she was, at that moment, fearful of saying anything although she, unlike me, fully comprehended the significance of the matter.

On the following morning we drove to the airport in Atlanta because Susan was arriving to attend the funeral.

The funeral service was conducted at the funeral home by the Rev. Wesley. He delivered a magnificent message and stated we might never know the why of this radical occurrence in our lifetime on this earth.

Doc's sister was so loving and gracious. She had taken pictures of the casket and gave me several. I also gave Doc's brother a few of Doc's belongings.

We then spoke with some of Doc's relatives who expressed the hope that Doc's father would not make an appearance. Why?

Chapter Sixteen

On the drive back home, my heart, soul, and mind were enmeshed in a shroud of deep gloom.

Suddenly, I became very excited. There, in the dark of night, was Doc, standing on the side of the road, tall and stately. His magnificent build was arrayed in white robes from head to foot.

I turned to Kris and exclaimed, "Did you see, did you see that?" It seemed no one in the car responded. Kris gently told me to calm down.

Back in my apartment at the Regency Club, much apprehension manifested itself once again. There were many questions and no plausible answers. A saving grace was my job. I received a great deal of needed support. Also, having to deal with students' problems gave me a measure of relief from my own situation. It was the "alone-again" syndrome that was torture.

Each time I started my car proved to be traumatic as a bit of paranoia set in. Due to the mystery surrounding the murder, I guess I fully expected it could be bombed and might explode. I also suspected that I was being watched and followed. Several weeks of this atmosphere of fear, which felt like a vice closing in on me, had elapsed when suddenly I felt very safe. It was as though an invisible divine cordon of angels was surrounding me. I knew nothing could penetrate this protective force. My personal self was now safe and secure.

Very often I would spend a night in the country at Susan's home. On one occasion I was awakened during the night with a headache, the dull ache concentrated in the center of my forehead. I fell back to sleep and dreamed. In the dream I was standing at the foot of the bed fully dressed. The bed was made, and Doc was walking up the stairs naked, tall and stately, and he looked marvelous. He was physically perfect, and the skin on his entire body reflected a light golden glow.

All the next day I kept this vision intact within my mind, and the dream warmed my heart. I felt secretly and deliciously happy and did not share this experience with anyone. Doc had said he would return to me, and he did, in spirit and dreams.

However, just one day of this unspeakable joy was not enough to sustain me. It was a temporary relief from the burden which had been weighing heavily on my heart and mind. Despite the fact of this exquisite, ephemeral cloak that the apparition of the dream provided, I soon slipped back into the Land of Nod, fumbling with the noxious fumes of sadness.

Several weeks later I again dreamed Doc was at the apartment door. I excitedly said, "I'm coming." I got to the door to remove the chain lock and chair I used as a barricade, when suddenly I knew there was no need to open the door as all was still.

Much later, I dreamed I was in another place, possibly Georgia, and Doc was there. It was a motel room in a country setting. There was a person there representing the law, although without uniform. Also, my brother Jules was there and reading a letter I had composed for mailing. My brother was advising me to delete one sentence from the letter. I then pulled the drapery aside and looked out on a sea of trees.

Dealing with facts and facing them is perhaps far easier, no matter what they may be, than inventing theories to explain a set of circumstances. Of course, facing incomprehensible fears without facts is sheer misery.

Why was Doc kidnapped? Why was he driven to a pasture at midnight and murdered execution style? Why was he shot at close range, his head blown off. Who, in fact, did it? Why did the police say they were holding a federal parolee for trial but refuse to release his name?

At this point, I decided to call the F.B.I. office and ask if they could help. My reasoning powers led me to conclude that since the murder took place in a different state and, in addition, a federal parolee was being held – surely the federal government could assist.

The agent I spoke to on the phone listened to my explanations without asking my name then firmly, but politely, said, "I'm sorry, lady, but this is just another murder."

Just another murder? What was our society deteriorating to when murder was nothing? This was my husband the agent was referring to. A human life had been destroyed. This reply seemed so blatantly irresponsible. This voice on the phone, so very casual about my tragedy, did this voice connect to a person without feelings? Perhaps the line from a poem that kept running through my head was prophetic, "I bargained with life for a penny, and life would pay no more." This agent did not even ask my name.

Chapter Seventeen

My car was packed with all my favorite clothing and my very best luggage in anticipation of a weekend trip to visit Kris's family in central Florida. On Friday, the day I was to leave directly after work, I stepped out of my classroom at break time to discover all my belongings stolen from my car, including my C.B. radio and Misty Harbor coat. This was another disappointment to be dealt with, but, as a friend said, "You are lucky they didn't take your car."

A few days later as I was viewing the news on television, a program regarding help for victims of crime was explained. The program was in conjunction with the State Attorney's office and was called Victim Witness Aid. Was I not the victim of a crime?

The following day I called the State Attorney's office to explain my predicament. I was given an appointment, and this is when I met Sandy Dunbar, a specialist in criminology. This was the beginning of some important support that I needed very much, as well the beginning of a very special friendship.

Sandy checked out my stolen property from a list I compiled consisting of a complete description of the articles. However, she was amazed at the amount of items in the room where the police allowed her to look. Sandy decided it was an impossible task to determine if any of my stolen articles were in this conglomeration. Sandy became a guardian angel to me. She helped me through the many aspects concerning the murder that were to follow.

Murder is so repulsive and definitely difficult to come to terms with when it happens to someone so close. One expression of sympathy that I treasured came from my cousin

Marie, Aunt Lydia's daughter. In part, she stated, "I just want you to know I have been thinking about you almost constantly since I was told the shocking and tragic news last weekend about Doc. It must be awful for you. I hope it won't be too long before you will be able to cherish the good memories and put the bad ones out of your mind and out of your dreams. I have a sort of personal motto in which I try to find the good in everything, but the only good I can find in this is that you will no doubt be a stronger person for having endured this, as you are still young and lovely and can have a beautiful life ahead of you if you let yourself and are cautious. What else can I say to comfort you? I don't know, but I know that I think of you with love." This succinctly worded message I believe was the way most people felt.

All through the period of time following the murder, I was seeking to employ escape methods for myself. I tried to air much of my frustration by changing my hair. I assumed an entirely different hairstyle, an "Afro," that was a wash-and-shake permanent. It was a totally different look for me. Since my naturally curly hair had never been permed before, it was different. My family didn't like it.

But what was important to me was that I felt different. The students in our program loved it, although they were surprised by the change. Also, I began to try all different shades of color in my hair. On a Saturday I spent the entire day just redoing my hair shades. This, of course, was a dreadful way to cope.

On the other hand, going to the beach was an activity that proved therapeutic. I would lie in the sun for hours and relive my life with Doc. This was the same beach where Doc and I had spent much time together. However, now I was alone again.

Chapter Eighteen

A series of communications began with police personnel in Georgia. Sandy Dunbar called the sheriff's office in the county where the murder took place, explaining her position in assisting me. In this conversation she requested a death certificate, the coroner's report, a list of the deceased's property being held, and the defendant's name as well as a tentative trial date.

We received the death certificate, but no listing of the property being held in evidence. My name as recorded on the certificate was inaccurate. Sandy made another request for the missing information. Also, in a phone conversation, Sgt. Adelson told me that a fire had burned Granny's home a few days before the murder – this was the same home where Doc was living at the time of the crime. Sandy wrote to the fire department requesting a report of the fire. A few days later a short note, written on a half-sheet of lined yellow paper, was received. The note stated "we are not able to find a fire report on this date at this address. We will need more information." More mystery and confusion.

A letter which I received from Sgt. Adelson contained a check for $23.47. Sgt. Adelson explained the check was issued by Wayne's Sanitation and was a payroll check for the last day Doc had worked. The Sgt. explained it had been in his file for some time and he decided he should release it to me. Sgt. Adelson further stated that he could not release any additional information to me, but I should feel free to call him with any questions.

The correspondence with Georgia officials was less than satisfactory. It was certainly true that if I had not had the help and cooperation that Sandy provided, I would have been kept in the dark concerning many aspects of the case.

After virtually months of practically no communication, I decided to write to Sgt. Adelson. In the letter I stated that due to the seeming lack of communication, I planned to travel to Georgia and speak to him personally. This resulted in a message to me through the local West Palm Beach police stating a trial was scheduled to begin in several months, and if I wished further information I should contact Sgt. Adelson. A few calls to him yielded no results. I tried again. Sgt. Adelson was not in. It was obvious that I was being ignored.

Next, I managed to speak to the D.A.'s secretary in Georgia. I asked if a transcript of the trial would be available to me. She replied that it would be but that I would have to pay for it. I agreed; however, she then stated it might not be possible in any case.

I immediately contacted Sandy Dunbar who, in turn, contacted officials in Georgia. They informed her that they had decided there had been no need to inform me as to the trial as I was not a witness.

The afternoon was spent trying to contact the district attorney and others in the county where the trial was to take place. It was difficult.

When I finally managed to speak with an assistant district attorney, he attempted to discourage me from attending the trial. He said there was only one motel in the area, and that it was decrepit. Also, for the first time I learned the defendant's name – Wilmer Joel. Wilmer Joel was charged with kidnapping, murder, and possession of firearms.

Once again I contacted the district attorney's office and related the incident I had experienced on our honeymoon in Chattanooga, Tennessee, namely the threat Doc had received to "get out of town or you will be shot." The district attorney seemed to attribute some significance to this event and stated that I should come to the trial as a witness and would be called on only if it should become necessary for them to use my testimony.

Again, my local state attorney's office came to my assistance, and Sandy Dunbar was instrumental in making arrangements for me to go to the trial. She arranged transportation to the airport and asked me to call her when I arrived in Georgia. She said that if she were in my place, she would certainly want to be there and see that justice was done to the perpetrator of this heinous crime.

Chapter Nineteen

I arrived at the Atlanta airport at 10:00 a.m. Two persons were to meet me as I had been promised as much protection as possible; however, there was no one at the gate so I decided to recover my baggage when I noticed two young guys standing off to the side.

Sgt. Adelson, with his assistant, recognized me. I soon realized I was thinking of them as a "Freebie and the Bean" equivalent. My two escorts drove me to a Howard Johnson's motel where they had secured a room for me. On this drive I sat in the back seat. I soon realized they seemed to feel terribly inconven-ienced by me. I also sensed they felt I was totally unnecessary to the case.

Sgt. Adelson began questioning me, trying to find out who I might know of Doc's acquaintances in Georgia, all the while speaking to one another in the front seat as though I were a "nonperson." This attitude turned me off and there-fore I answered with brief, non-commital sentences. At this point they decided I didn't "know anything." However, in my purse were many little evidences (proofs) of Doc's life, but I was not about to volunteer anything as, after all, they had already predetermined my ignorance.

We arrived at the motel and after they escorted me to my room, Sgt. Adelson told me they would call me the next day and inform me as to when I should come to the trial.

In the morning I was informed via telephone that transportation would not be available to me. It was suggested that I hire a taxi which they would call for me. I was then told it wasn't necessary for me to be there that day as jury selection was taking place.

In the meantime I learned that I was a great distance

from the courthouse. I also learned the taxi fare would be approximately thirty dollars. I knew I must get to the courthouse. I then found a car rental agency and hired a car using my Visa card. My cash funds were extremely limited at this point.

It was late morning when I started out. My hair was clipped short as in my frustration after the Afro hairdo, a hairdresser managed to damage my hair. Again in this, my "new" frustrating situation, I was unhappy with my hair, and it had been clipped extremely short. On the way to the courthouse I found a walk-in beauty shop and had my hair washed and set. I did have a great tan, and I was wearing a very pretty dress. The dress had a white eyelet top with a square neck and full three-quarter sleeves. The waistline was fitted with a lovely blue print skirt and a ruffled edging of white eyelet at the bottom. I did know the importance of a good first impression, and I gave it my best shot.

When I arrived at the courthouse, a few people were surprised that I had taken the initiative in spite of their instructions. Also, I soon became aware that had I not done so, I would have missed the entire trial.

I spoke with the district attorney briefly as a recess was in progress when I arrived. Since his secretary had informed me previously by phone that I should bring my marriage certificate, I tried to show it to her. In addition, I had with me an album of wedding pictures and other documentation. When I approached her with this "proof," she merely stated that it was not necessary. I wondered why I had been requested to bring anything at all.

Chapter Twenty

There were various family members seated in a small room. They were Doc's "kin" and had some interesting things to tell me.

The trial had begun and was in progress when I entered the courtroom. I sat down. The judge had been informed that I was in attendance. The judge made a statement duly noting the presence of Mrs. James Foxx in the courtroom, and I stood up in acknowledgment. Doc's mother came and sat beside me. She seemed very happy to see me. She whispered that she hoped Wilmer Joel, the defendant, would get the electric chair. My thoughts were not too coherent, and I honestly did not know my feelings at this time or what I thought at this moment in time.

The jurors were 12 men who appeared to be very "country" and very strong. I liked the judge.

Wilmer Joel was on the stand and being questioned. Didn't he go around threatening to blow James' f. . .ing head off for $10,000.00 owed him? This and much, much, more of the same line of questioning. The questioning had to be deftly handled as there were aspects of this case that could conceivably be another entire matter. Seated there looking at the defendant, I began to realize he was indeed the perpetrator of the honeymoon threat. Only now he had a short, neat, business-style haircut. He also had on clothing that would be considered proper business attire. However, in my mind I pictured him as he was dressed on that day in Chattanooga, and, indeed, it was the same person in different dress.

Wilmer Joel's wife was being questioned. It was revealed that she had to be brought to the trial from jail where she was being held for robbing a bank.

Didn't she assist in the crime? There was evidence that she had knowledge of the gun. Didn't she, with her father, break up the gun used in this crime and then put the pieces in the dump? The evidence also consisted of a tape-recording saying "there are pieces here, pieces there, pieces everywhere" in reference to the gun. The witness denied that she had any knowledge of the gun; however, clever questioning revealed the fact that she indeed did have knowledge of the gun and its subsequent disposal.

When the defendant's little girl was placed on the stand for verification of her parents' possession of the gun, I was horrified. For then, in the face of this child, I saw the stark reality of the many innocent people affected by this crime, a crime which encircled with insidious fingers to harm a multitude of the blameless.

During a short break I spoke to the D.A. and asked for clarification of some points brought out in court testimony. I explained that it would help to have facts because I could deal with facts, as theories and suppositions were vague and elusive and therefore difficult to handle. He replied that while the trial was in session he was not free to discuss issues but that he would give me all I might request after the trial.

Testimony during the trial revealed that Doc had been carrying a heavy chain around with him for protection, but no guns. He definitely had reason to be fearful.

The fire at Granny's house was mentioned. Doc had been wearing sneakers when murdered, something I had never known him to do. I met a salesperson in the waiting room who told me she had been summoned as a witness as she had sold Doc the clothing he was wearing when he was murdered, the clothing necessary to replace that lost in the fire. This person was a lovely dark woman who was extremely interested in the picture album I had with me.

I had missed the testimony of Patti Thornton, the state's star witness. She had testified that Doc had been taken at gunpoint from her home (next to Granny's) on the evening he was last seen alive. There were several people present. Instead of calling the police, Patti went to the store and calmly purchased a six pack of beer.

This was another phase of the trial. Who was Patti Thornton involved with and why?

During a recess I met Patti Thornton in the hallway. She had long black hair and blue eyes. To me, she appeared to be strung out. I was showing her the pictures in my wedding album when Sgt. Adelson reached out and closed the book. He said I mustn't show Patti the pictures as she was the state's witness.

At this point, Patti joined me for coffee at a local Dairy Queen. I found myself feeling sorry for Patti. In turning state's witness, she was afraid of being murdered. Why? What exactly were the mysterious circumstances, the other aspects of the case? Patti also told me she did not know why she did not call the police and had entertained a boyfriend instead. Also, Patti stated that she was making plans to marry Doc. When I asked her how that was possible as he was already married, it was clear that she had not considered this fact.

Upon returning to the courtroom for summations, I listened as the defense attorney was making a plea for mercy.

Next, the D.A. in his summation said, "Did Wilmer Joel allow for mercy when he forced James to his knees and shot his head off? Did he allow James to pray before the deed was committed?" Picturing the scene made my heart ache, and I cried.

The jurors went out to deliberate. Soon there was a commotion as a new development arose. No one was allowed in the courtroom except the judge, attorneys, and jurors. It seemed the defendant remembered something he wanted to relay at this time.

In the hallway outside the courtroom, scoffing remarks were made to the effect that naturally the defendant would try anything to save his life. It was obviously a last-ditch effort on Wilmer Joel's part.

I then went downstairs and talked with a man employed in the courthouse. When I remarked as to what a fine building the courthouse was, he said it was built recently as the previous building had been burned. It seems there were those who wanted to destroy the files and records contained in the building. The irony is that everything had been burned except the files and records. The arson technique seemed to be quite fashionable in Georgia.

It was time to return to the courtroom. Everyone was seated and the jurors filed in and were seated. As the judge polled the jurors, each one without exception stood and said, "Guilty." It was without a doubt a unanimous decision.

The judge then passed sentence for the electric chair and said, "May God have mercy on your soul."

Chapter Twenty-One

Suddenly I felt quite lost and really wanted to get back to South Florida. Outside the courtroom I saw Sgt. Adelson holding the car door open for Patti Thornton. He was evidently responsible for her transportation, I thought as I walked to my rental car.

After I arrived at my motel, I called Sandy Dunbar. She was very relieved to hear from me. She then said she had been very worried about me. It seems the law has access to information that can't be divulged to the layman.

The next day on the plane ride home I wrote a long letter to Sgt. Adelson which covered a range of my thoughts and feelings which could not be measured. Fate seems cruel and strange and unfair. I did not, however, mail this letter.

Since I had decided to move, once I returned to my apartment I continued my packing. What would I do next?

I received a letter from June and Bob who were in Connecticut for the summer. June wrote, "We had the idea you would be making some sort of change this summer. Bob and I talked of it and came to the conclusion that it would probably be best for you if you did change apartments, jobs, towns, etc. You have had such a miserable period in your life to walk through; it seems a complete change could help put it behind you. I know that 'out of sight is not out of mind,' but it is better than looking at it all the time. I know it would be hard to leave that lovely apartment, but the association you can really do without. You know how someone can mull things over, twisting and turning things around while someone else can see the quick solution." June's words were so true. Unfortunately, a fast or easy solution was seemingly impossible.

In seeking new living quarters, I explored the area up and down the Palm Beach County coastline. I thought the first choice was going to be an ideal solution. It was a one-room, very small and fifty dollars a week. In the course of my packing I had sold many of my accumulated "treasures." There were still many things to put in storage. This one-room deal, I realized very quickly, would be disastrous, and I did not spend one night there. Of course, my deposit was not refunded.

This began a series of searches which ended when I took an apartment in Delray Beach. It would be for three months, only until the lucrative season arrived. When I called the number in the advertisement for this place, a frightened voice responded. There was a hurricane warning in the area at this time, and this voice announced that the hurricane would strike at precisely 6:00 a.m. the following morning. I laughed at the preciseness in this statement and said, "Really, how do you know?" The voice answered "Because I heard it on the news." In spite of this, I located the place and secured the apartment.

Once again, I piled everything I could into my Monte Carlo and started moving. It took several trips. Fortunately the brunt of the hurricane did not hit this part of the coast as I moved into this beach efficiency apartment. It was neat, really small with a small bathroom and closet-like kitchen. Although I could scarcely move in this place, I felt strangely content.

The apartment building was interesting, a small garden type with plenty of space around it. The landlady owner was the most interesting feature. She freely roamed in and through the apartments at random (when the tenants were not home) watching TV or whatever. She was constantly moving furniture and her apartment was the only one on the second level which was heaped to capacity with everything imaginable. In conversation with her I often was surprised to find myself laughing again. She had such a humorous way of telling tales.

Every opportunity I had I was on the beach, walking and gathering shells. A part deep inside me identified with the broken shells on the sand. Resting my mind in this beautiful beach setting was indeed therapeutic.

Chapter Twenty-Two

At the time Doc left town I had begun taking classes again at Broward Community College, returning to the education I had dropped due to the honeymoon and marriage. However, I re-entered the college scene electing to complete and earn my degree. I recalled that my oldest daughter, on a visit just after Doc left, encouraged me to complete a research paper I was working on and to continue with my classes. When I thought I couldn't – I did – and graduated about a year later, receiving an A.A. degree with honors.

I then registered at FAU in Boca Raton to continue my education. Because I had never lost my taste for the school campus, it was very good for me. Yet, the empty moments were always there. The aloneness in spite of the activities of work and school and friends was ever my companion. At college, I joined the alumni chapter of the honor society I was a member of at BCC. This activity was interesting and many good friends were the result, as well as banquets, dances, and other events such as civic volunteer work, all sponsored by the fraternity.

When November rolled around, I had to move from my little haven. I thought back to the first day I moved in and recalled lying on the bed, actually more like a cot, with the TV at the foot of the bed and thinking, okay this is it. Make the best of it. Then as I was about to fall asleep, a program on TV featuring Fast Freddie, a male stripper, caused my eyes to react with wide-eyed wonder.

It was November and the landlady said she could get double the rent during the winter as well as having her regular winter residents returning. Therefore, I should make plans to move.

Susan and Larry arrived the following rainy Saturday afternoon in their yellow pick-up truck and moved me to their home in the country. Susan very graciously said, "Just think of it as visiting us for the holidays."

Traveling to work and to college once again took on a new dimension and a different direction. There was a lot of commuting involved. I spent a great deal of time in my Monte Carlo. My dear friend Jan, with whom I had become acquainted just prior to Doc's death, was always ready to listen and make me welcome at her home with many fun, impromptu parties and social events going on in her group. These were numerous and included celebrations for both finding and losing a job.

Being with Susan and Larry was a comfort zone. And yet I was still groping and hurting. Would I ever really get any answers? Was Doc, in fact, dead? Since I was denied the right to view his body, this thought continued to haunt me.

After the holidays I began to feel I had taken up enough space where I was living and thought it was time to move on. Once again, I was considering another place to live, but where? Then, out of the blue, I received a phone call one evening from a teacher I worked with in the school program, telling me of a place. She said it was a house in Lantana and the folks that lived there were returning to Indiana for six months, and she thought I should talk to them about renting the house. I did, and as a result met a delightful couple who raised bees in Indiana. It was a pleasant meeting, and I liked them immediately. The house was charming.

The furnishings were comfortable, and there was a nice fence-enclosed backyard with lovely shrubs that gave total privacy. It was just a short walk to the beach across the Intracoastal Waterway bridge. This began yet another labyrinth passage in my life.

I soon had a network of friends. There was Jeff, living on Ocean Avenue in a room in a small motel. Just across the street on the next corner of this same avenue living in a small house was Mike. I don't know if they were acquainted at all but they both became my friends. There was also a minister in a church next door to me that was housed in a brick building that did not much resemble a church. Actually I just had a nodding acquaintance with the good reverend. In fact, there was very little activity in this place, and the minister had living quarters in the rear of the building.

There was also a person named Karen across the street who strung together the words for advertising that airplanes displayed flying along the beaches. Karen was nice, and I enjoyed talking with her. The house on the other side of mine was totally closed up for the summer months. Other than that, there were mainly small wood-framed homes or small concrete-block homes in the neighborhood.

Lantana is a charming town with much small-town flavor and is home to many Finnish families. I lived east of South Dixie Highway, which runs through the town. The railroad tracks are parallel to Dixie just to the west. There are a few stores and restaurants and also a post office and a bank. I enjoyed going to a few of these places, as some of the restaurants had good food and entertainment. Soon I developed the habit of walking to the beach. At times Jeff would walk with me. Jeff was fun, and he went as far as to borrow a motorcycle and ride along side of me as I walked. He would then proceed to do stunts with the bike to try and impress me. Jeff had a lot of charm and had a muscular build as well as very blue eyes, dark curly hair, and a mustache.

Several weeks after I met Jeff, he asked me to go to a theater. I preferred an indoor air-conditioned place, but Jeff insisted on seeing Cheech and Chong – who he said were fabulous – at an outdoor theater. Well, Jeff promptly fell sound asleep as soon as the film started, and I was totally bored with the movie. It was just a short drive along the Intracoastal Waterway and on the way home, a police officer pulled me over for misjudging a traffic light. After a routine check, the officer returned and spoke to me very pleasantly. As we drove away, Jeff said, "I knew he wouldn't give you a ticket, all he gave you was a lecture, and did you see the huge diamond he was wearing?" It seems Jeff had his license revoked for what he said was a minor infraction.

A few weeks later as I was returning from grocery shopping on a Saturday morning, Jeff ran alongside my car as I turned the corner.. He wanted me to stop. However, it was only a short distance from my driveway so I kept moving and turned into the drive. When I got out of the car Jeff said, "Do you mind if I ask you a question?"

I replied, "Of course not, what is it?"

And then Jeff said, "You're a healthy middle-aged woman. Would you consider having an affair with me?"

I laughed and then said, "Well, Jeff, at the moment I'm going to have a healthy lunch and then take a sun bath."

"You're going to what? You mean you're not mad?"

I said, "No, of course not." It seems Jeff really expected me to be angry.

On the other hand, Mike would often come over in the evening, and we would have pleasant conversations. Once I gave Mike a foot rub. I had been interested in hand and foot reflexology since I read an article about it in a magazine. Since then I had acquired books on this science and became very good at it, and I have done this for many people at various times, always gratis. My daughter Susan was my most ardent "customer." The other members of my family followed a close second.

Mike was nice looking and a good person to know. It proved to be a nice, easy friendship. But he had this thing about seeing me in a bathing suit, perhaps because I didn't hang around in one. Yet one day when I was sun bathing in the privacy of my back yard, he walked in on me. My suit was quite brief, and I dared not move until he left. Of course he stayed and talked for a long time. He then said, "you look great." He couldn't understand why I was shy about his seeing me in a suit. Neither did I. This nonetheless was a minor or moot question.

The things I could not truly understand were many unanswered questions that the law failed to respond to, such as the correspondence that was so polite but noncommital that I received from Georgia, and the inventory held by the police concerning Doc's belongings that were unattainable. Actually, I was given no satisfaction concerning the inventory, so I resorted to enlisting the assistance of a person who was an editor of a national weekly magazine. It was only when this person threatened publication of the situation that I was supplied with a list of the inventory. These items were promised to me after the trial for at this time I was told they could be released. This became yet another unfulfilled situation resulting in more frustration.

Chapter Twenty-Three

Seeking answers and a measure of peace, I, of course, relied on my faith. In spite of this, one day I called a person advertised as a "psychic reader." This was partly born of my curiosity about this science. As I spoke with her on the phone I asked her if she could pick up on any particular "vibes" in my voice. The husky voice said I would have to come and see her. That afternoon, on my way to a luau at Susan's house, I stopped at the house with the big sign displaying the palm of a hand, declaring a reader lived here. I was ushered in through a long hallway and turned left into another hallway lined with seats on either side. I sat down and this reader sat beside me.

We did not face each other and that felt awkward. I was expected to do all the talking. When I said I thought she would give me some insight, she said something about my needing a man and that's what I should strive for. She then made a few more remarks that were vague and inconsequential. She then announced that the time was up. Since the $25.00 fee had been collected in advance, I expressed my disappointment and said I thought that it was a rather brief meeting. The reply was that for extra money, candles would be lit in church for me. The meeting was terminated.

Back in my car, I was headed west for the luau when the thought "there is one born every minute" crossed my mind. I promptly turned my car around and headed back to the reader's house. I walked up to the door and knocked. When the door was opened, I told the reader I felt I had not received full value for my money. With this, she returned half the money from a pocket in her dress. "You are a bad woman. That's why you have so many troubles," she said in her husky voice. I then went on to the luau, which I found to be most enjoyable.

Again my mind was tugging away on the subject of Wilmer Joel. Why? It was disturbing to me. I had written to the district attorney some weeks ago requesting the present status of the subject, but I had not received a reply. Once more I prevailed upon Sandy Dunbar, telling her that this weighed heavily on my mind. I asked her to find out if Wilmer Joel was incarcerated or exactly what his status was at the present time. Sandy called the county superior court and was transferred to records. Sandy learned that Wilmer Joel, who had been on death row in Georgia awaiting the governor's order for execution, had been transferred to another prison.

When I heard the news, I became very upset. Sandy Dunbar said she was extremely upset by the news as well. Sandy also told me this is the way it had to be and nothing could be done about it. Sandy also said that she thought I must be psychic to have had such strong feelings about this situation. I later learned that the prison he had been transferred to was where the new electric chair was housed.

Shortly after this I began hearing advertisements for a psychic fair to be held at the Delray Beach Mall. This held a strong attraction for me, although I felt I did not place any real faith in it. At the same time the fair was being advertised, I heard, on my car radio, ministers in the area warning against the nature of this phenomena. My curiosity and interest had peaked and on Saturday morning I headed for the mall. As I casually walked among the tables set up inside the mall, checking the surroundings, I became apprehensive. There were people seated at tables receiving predictions and/or advice, and all seemed engrossed.

Finally, I summoned up the courage to inquire as to the cost, which I learned depended on the length of time, etc.

Twenty dollars was the least you could pay. My funds were
extremely low, and I felt I couldn't afford this. I left the mall
and went to my car and began checking my resources. Somehow I managed to produce the necessary funds and boldly
walked back to the fair. After all, was I not desirous of seeking
answers and hopeful of receiving solutions here?

Soon I was seated, and the medium opposite me said,
"I see much sorrow and tears around you." She then took
my hands, and I felt a tremendous vibration soar through me.
Next, with closed eyes and her face upturned, she related there
was an answer to the tragedy I had experienced. There was no
personal danger to my person, however, as she saw angels all
around me, protecting me. Also she stated there was a key to
a box, either a post office box or a bank box that held something valuable. I see, she went on, a small brown paper bag
filled with white powder and a man stapling the bag. This bag
was contained in the box and there was a small paper with two
signatures on it and the paper was very valuable. This, she
said, is worth a great deal of money. The medium seemed to
think I should have knowledge of these items. I said, "There
is no paper that I'm aware of." She looked bewildered, and
said I should look very carefully for this paper.

Doc had many keys, which I assumed belonged to the
equipment he used on various jobs. I had disposed of most
of them as they had no meaning for me. The building the alleged box was presumed to be in was described to me. It was,
indeed, she said, in Georgia, just above the Florida border.

When I heard "white powder," my reaction was one
of alarm. Certainly I had no desire to find this bag, even if I
conceivably could.

Chapter Twenty-Four

Once again I moved for the winter season and then back again to the house in Lantana after the owners of the house once again returned to Indiana. They were so delightful and also happy to have me as a tenant. They again gave me a good supply of honey.

To me, it was rather like returning home, albeit temporarily. After I had settled in, I chose a Sunday afternoon to drive the short distance to visit my brother Bob and his wife, June. They invited me to go to dinner with them at the Bahama Shack and said the catfish served there was great. I agreed to go, and we enjoyed a great dinner. Upon my return home, my house was in darkness. Since I had planned to be home before dark, I had not left a light on. As I entered the kitchen, I noticed the door had been tampered with. This frightened me, and I called the police. They agreed that an attempt to break in was evident. The minister who lived next door said he heard a strange noise coming from my back yard and turned on a light, and when he did so, the noise stopped.

Four days later the police arrested two men as they attempted to break in the house to the north of me. The incident was reported on TV and in the newspapers. Evidently the police had trailed the automobile used by the offenders in unmarked police cars and by helicopter all the way from Miami Beach. Shortly after this, a detective was at my door and asked if he could speak with me. I said, of course, I very much want to talk to someone about this. The detective said it was felt the intention was to break into the house where I was living. He went on to say they could not understand why these men would drive the distance from Miami Beach to Lantana, passing wealthy homes and expensive condos all the way, while they held pass keys that would take them into any house or building. The fact that my neighborhood was less than wealthy and there was nothing of great value here was puzzling to the authorities. The detective did say it was thought I had something the men were looking for. What and why? Once again, no one was answering or even second guessing with any kind of logic I could understand.

Questions I did not ask were, what could they want from me? How did the police know to follow these men on this particular day? Why were these men held on $50,000.00 bonds? And months later, why were they still being held?

There is a stigma attached to being victimized in a circumstance of murder, no matter how innocent one may be. One thing I learned is that whether consciously or unconsciously, it dictates a certain, perhaps illogical, reaction to one's life. Also, with the attempted break-in, I felt extremely fearful in this charming little house. The owners, very kindly, with no questions asked, installed a new door with better locks. Yet I still felt I must move. The next move was to a dormitory room at FAU where I had acquired a position in the admissions office and was taking courses in the evening to earn my B.A. degree. My friend Jan and her husband, Tony, came one evening in their van and moved me to the campus in Boca Raton.

This was the beginning of a new phase in my life with yet another view. I adapted quickly to campus life and made many friends. I truly love academia and the acceptance I found there.

In retrospect, so much had happened in the month of February. It was in this same month that I met Doc and in this month that Doc had died.

Ironically, one early Sunday morning in February, as I was walking on Delray Beach, I saw something that I knew to be symbolic for me. A landmark building was in a heap of wood and mortar as the razing of the building was in its final stages. This structure was located on the corner of Atlantic Avenue and North Ocean Boulevard. The destruction was accomplished to make way for a new and modern edifice.

In essence, it equaled my experience, for who is to say what memories were demolished in this destruction, now rubble, which seemed to parallel my life. I must turn the page to a blank one and try to begin again.

The symbolism the building portrayed to me was just the semblance of an idea, for the structure was engineered with wood and stone and steel, whereas my temple consists of flesh and blood and feelings, thought, and spirit. It breathes and moves. Begin again? It is time for yet another pilgrimage.

As the ancient Mahabharata states, "Time is the seed of the universe."

The End

The End